# Early Pennine Settlement

Printed and bound in Great Britain by
FRETWELL & BRIAN LTD.
Silsden, Nr. Keighley, Yorkshire.

11s
(55p)

INGLEBOROUGH FROM CHAPEL-LE-DALE
*The north-western aspect of the hill fort
is seen from the former Roman road.*

# Early Pennine Settlement

### A Field Study by
## Alan King

*A Romano-British disc brooch*

DALESMAN PUBLISHING COMPANY, LTD.,
CLAPHAM (YORKSHIRE),
VIA LANCASTER
1970

**ATTERMIRE AND THE SCARS**
Block faulted limestone topography.

# *Preface*

MANY will be familiar with the geology and also the natural vegetation of the Pennines, possibly from Dr. Raistrick and the late Mr. John Illingworth's *The Face of North West Yorkshire*. Here it is hoped to stimulate an interest in those features of the landscape that are the result of man's use of the land over the last 10,000 years. An attempt is being made to give an appreciation of the native economies and the effect that has been made on these by immigrant and conquering forces, at least until the end of prehistoric time, from the field evidence and from a study of the many museum finds.

Readers will already have an interest in the district and so I hope they will excuse my stressing the point that almost every site mentioned in the text is on private land. Rarely are they crossed by or bordered by footpaths. Please do get permission to visit the sites, checking perhaps at the same time the whereabouts of the bull.

May I thank all the landowners who have allowed me to survey and excavate on their land and who have so often pointed out details I would otherwise have missed. Many museum curators have also helped a great deal and for their help I am most grateful. Being always amazed by the size of the collection and variety of the finds in the Pig Yard Club Museum at Settle, I must thank Tom Lord in particular for spending so much time encouraging and answering my questions.

*A bone-handled iron knife from Victoria Cave.*
*(British Museum)*

# Contents

# Illustrations

*Photographs on pages 63, 74, 75 by J. K. St. Joseph (Crown Copyright); 86 upper, by courtesy of the Trustees of the British Museum; 86 lower, by courtesy of the Curator, Tullie House, Carlisle; 12 by C. H. Wood, Bradford; 15 by Horners (K. and J. Jelley), Settle; 29 and 30 by permission of the Curator, Craven Museum, Skipton. All illustrations where no museum location is stated are housed in the Pig Yard Club Collection at Settle and are used with warm acknowledgement to Mr. Thomas Lord.*
*All uncredited photographs by the author.*
*Cover painting and reconstructions, together with some of the drawings, by Celia M. King.*

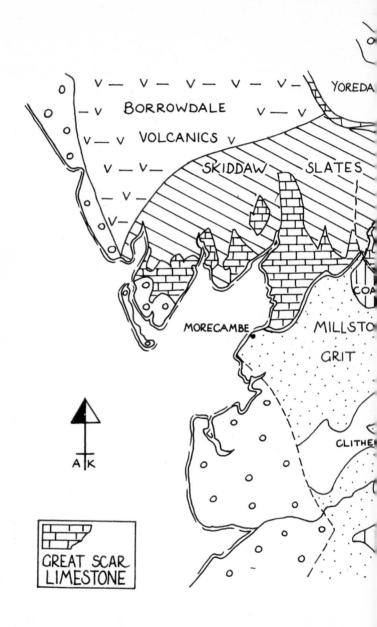

GEOLOGICAL S

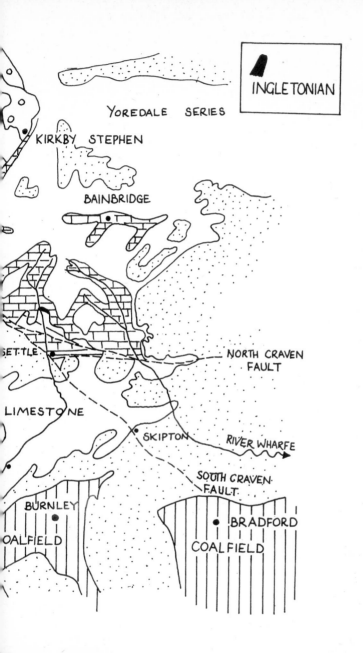

INGLETONIAN

YOREDALE  SERIES

KIRKBY  STEPHEN

BAINBRIDGE

SETTLE

NORTH CRAVEN
FAULT

LIMESTONE

SKIPTON

RIVER WHARFE

SOUTH CRAVEN
FAULT

BURNLEY

COALFIELD

BRADFORD

COALFIELD

TCH  MAP

# 1. Geography and Environment

THE region under consideration is a portion of the Central Pennines, the westernmost part of the West Riding; it is largely situated in the Yorkshire Dales National Park. Within easy travelling distance of both the Yorkshire and Lancashire conurbations, this region is famous both as a scenic tourist area and as ground well-trodden by multitudes of students doing fieldwork in a variety of subjects.

An upland area with Millstone Grit capping most of the hills from Whernside (2,414 feet) to Great Whernside (2,310 feet), it is never the less considered a district of classic limestone scenery. The Great Scar Limestone stands bare, gaunt and almost level at about 1,150 feet. It stretches away beyond Malham to Grassington dipping beneath the Millstone Grit to the east. The Dent Fault in the west is the junction between the limestone and the Lower Palaeozoic shales and mudstones; the A65 from Settle to Ingleton runs along the foot of a series of escarpments best seen in the Buckhaw Brow neighbourhood.

To the south of the Craven Faults are the Bowland Fells and Skipton-Clitheroe region, exhibiting more subdued topography and limestones of basin and reef facies. Comparisons can be made between the quarries at Horton or Giggleswick with those at Clitheroe and Skipton. The Lower Carboniferous sea was deeper and muddier to the south, the series being now at least 6,000 feet thick, while the Askrigg Block to the north of the faults was covered by shallower, clearer water resulting in less than 2,000 feet of limestone.

Many of the rivers have cut their valleys down below the base of the Carboniferous Limestone exposing inliers of earlier rocks. The Greta has exposed the Ingletonian Precambrian series of slates and greywackes between Ingleton and Chapelle-Dale.[1] The Ribble Valley between Helwith Bridge and Horton is floored by Silurian flags in the south, and by Ingletonian at Horton. Other small inliers of Lower Palaeozo-

10

ics are found in Clapdale, Crummackdale, Silverdale and flanking and flooring the southern part of Malham Tarn.

All but the higher hills were covered by ice of the last advance, and drift deposits are fairly extensive with a remarkably fresh appearance. Glacial erosion removed most of the weathered material from the valley sides, and this process is to some extent responsible for the terraced outcrops of the limestone hill slopes. There are extensive areas of drumlins around Ribblehead and also between Long Preston, Gargrave and Skipton—i.e. on the watershed between the Ribble and Aire. The flat-floored valleys of Upper Wharfedale and Littondale, of Ribblesdale, between Long Preston and Settle, and of Wensleydale between Aysgarth and Bainbridge, were the sites of moraine—dammed ribbon lakes, left behind after the ice retreat.[2] The cold conditions of the late Pleistocene slowly changed; solifluxion produced terracettes on the steeper slopes, with stoneless hummocks covering flat and gently sloping areas.

The climate is now cool and damp. Temperatures on the valley floors rise from about 38°F in January to 58°F in July, though February can often be the coldest month and the rainfall at low levels in the west is about 40 ins. per annum, decreasing to the east. On the limestone plateau and hilltops, winters are colder with snow falling and lying on the ground more frequently. In 1963, the coldest winter on record since 1740, snow lay for more than 70 days and at the Malham Tarn Field Centre ground frost was recorded on 155 days. The fells also have a heavier rainfall, usually between 50 ins. and 70 ins. per annum. Generally lambing time coincides with the initial growth of grass, when the temperature has risen above 42°F, and begins in the tributary valleys of the Lune and Ribble; it follows 14 to 21 days later at higher levels. Some quality breeding ewes winter on the turnip fields of Lancashire or the Vale of Eden, while others are fed on imported hay and other fodders in the district.

The fell tops are moorland areas of peat 10 to 20 feet thick. Peat, sphagnum moss and associated cotton grass produce a zone of very little agricultural value though sheep do find some summer grazing and grouse find August hazardous. Where the peat has been eroded there are thin, sandy, leached soils and in some localities Alpine assemblages. Lower fell and higher valley slopes are zones of rough pasture characterized by brown earth soils where the area has been cleared of trees and the soil profile truncated. In places the soils of what were obviously medieval crofts, have been eroded completely;

11

CELTIC FIELDS NEAR MALHAM COVE
*They can be seen above the elbow of the road.*
*In the lower part of the photograph are long*
*medieval strip fields, all being beneath 18th century*
*enclosure walls.*

podsolic features may be seen but not good podsol soils. The most dominant grasses are the bents, (*Agrostis sp.*) mat grass (*Nardus stricta*) and the purple moor grass (*Molinia caerulea*). Over-grazing will lead to the disappearance of *Agrostis* but *Molinia* must be grazed during its early growth in about late May if it is to be of any nutritional value to stock.

Limestone pavement remains bare unless there are pockets of drift soils. Where there is even a thin soil, the upper part is so well leached that shallow rooted acidophylious plants can be found growing besides calcicolous plants with more penetrating roots. Heather, reminiscent of gritstone moors, can be seen on almost bare pavement. Woodlands are rare on the limestone plateau but patches of ash can be found and these are considered regenerated areas. The patches of Juniper seen on Moughton Fell are most likely to be the residue of pine woodland.

Alluviated valley floors give the best grazing and the meadows provide some hay for winter, while supplementary turnip and pulped sugar beet is brought in from the Vale of York. In a purely pastoral district changes occur slowly and at the present there appears to be a swing away from milk production on some farms to more specialized intensive beef-rearing units.

With a great number of smallholdings, dating back to a time when the dales were self sufficient, some rationalization is needed, and the Rural Development Board has been set up possibly with this in mind. Afforestation could give farming an extra dimension in the future and halt the rural depopulation of young people, but the conifers will not recreate the scenes that our Celtic ancestors saw.

## Early Investigations.

IMPROVEMENTS in communications, particularly the turnpike roads, began to end a period of relative isolation for the Dales. Prior to the turnpike improvements the packhorses carried goods between towns and great droves of Highland cattle came on foot along the green lanes, to be sold at fairs held on the moors.

The Keighley to Kendal Turnpike Act was passed in 1753 and the Keighley to Skipton road was "ordered" in April, 1762. With such well-known families as the Farrers, Inglibys and Birkbecks involved, it is not surprising to read that the Settle to Long Preston improvement was one of the first to be completed, possibly as early as 1754.[3] Motorists on the A65 still follow this route and appreciate that it is a road at low level when they skirt the flooded river valley at Long Preston after a period of heavy rain. The earlier road climbs out of Long Preston reaching an altitude of over 1,000 ft. on Hunter Bark before descending into Settle. The neighbourhood was brought into closer contact with London and it was not long before references to the district were appearing in print.

Thomas Pennant thought little of Settle.[4] It was left to the Rev. J. Hutton to draw attention to features of the limestone scenery in his *Tour of the Caves* (1781). In this account we find one of the first references to things archaeological; "We passed a large heap of stones, called hurder . . . They were all small round sandy and gritty stones, and all the stones on the surface of the ground near them are limestone. No doubt they were tumuli of some deceased chieftains." This was very accurate observation and our interpretation would be little different; the tumuli are still intact on the limestone pavement.

The last of the Enclosure Acts affecting the district had been passed about the time of Hutton's tour and twenty years later, the West Riding was given its first Board of Agriculture Report. "At this place (Settle) we saw the finest grass we ever viewed . . . it was of greater value to them when kept in grass than when cultivated by the plough." Figures quoted however show all the parishes with varying acreages of arable, most of it sewn with oats. Grain was then imported from the corn market at Knaresborough, and none has been grown since, except for a short period during the 1914-18 war. But cattle and sheep rearing has continued on the hill slopes and fell tops, the fields and farms being separated one from the other by dry-stone walls. Rarely has a wall been built or removed since the first Ordnance Survey map was made in 1846.

It was not until 1838 that the archaeological importance of the local caves were recognised. In May of that year Michael Horner, apprentice plumber, discovered Victoria Cave by entering a small opening known as a Foxhole. He found a bronze fibula and showed it to his master, Joseph Jackson, who in the following years was able to collect from the cave floor a fine collection of Roman coins, brooches and bronze implements. Besides claiming the credit for the cave's discovery, he is supposed to have sold his collection to the British Museum for £20. These finds are now difficult to identify but some are illustrated in C. Roach Smith's *Collectanea Antiqua*.

Many caves in the district were subsequently searched and

VICTORIA CAVE, SETTLE
*A photograph printed from the original glass plate
taken in the spring of 1870, when the first excavation
began under the auspices of the British Association.*

15

some dug by local landowners. Reginald Farrer joined Joseph Jackson in digging Victoria Cave and they also worked in Dowkerbottom. In 1866 the Settle Cave committee was formed and this body received the support of the British Association. A major excavation of Victoria Cave was planned, and Professor W. Boyd Dawkins acted initially as the director, being succeeded by R. H. Tiddeman.[5]

Many individuals and a variety of groups such as the Austwick Field Club, Settle Naturalist and Antiquarian Society, The Pig Yard Club and the Upper Wharfedale Society have excavated and built up collections of finds, many of which can be seen in the Craven Museum at Skipton (where R. H. Tiddeman's fine fossil collection is also housed) and the Pig Yard Club Museum in Settle.

1. *It should be noted that no granite is exposed or quarried in the Greta Valley, but the term seems to have been used because of the number of fresh felspar crystals seen in the coarser rocks. Recent geomagnetic surveys suggest a granite mass forms the core of the Askrigg Block at a depth of possibly little more than a kilometre.*
2. *King, C. A. M.—"The Yorkshire Dales"* (1960).
3. *Brigg, J. J.—"The King's Highway in Craven"* (1927).
4. *Pennant, T.—"A Tour from Alston Moor to Harrowgate and Brimham Crags"* (1804).
5. *Dawkins, W. B.—"Cave Hunting"* (1874).
   *Another book useful for ecological background to the area is W. H. Pearsall's "Mountains and Moorland"* (1950).

# 2. The Arrival of Man

ABOUT one-tenth of the earth's land surface is covered with ice, but this proportion varies, and during the Pleistocene it increased to almost one-third. There were at least two periods of refrigeration before the Pleistocene and these major glacial spells are not made up of uniform cold; they are interupted by interglacials, periods of warmer temperatures. The growth and retreat of the ice masses can be envisaged as being controlled by temperature change. Glaciers, unlike rivers do not have to obey the laws of gravity and run downhill. A sheet of ice 1,500 ft. thick can pick up boulders from the floor of Crummackdale and deposit them at a higher level on the valley side or on the limestone plateau.

With large quantities of ice on the land, sea level would be lower (our Junior School "Water Cycle" would be broken). Other changes of land levels relative to sea levels would also occur, but it is not intended to discuss these. It is sufficient to point out that the North Sea and English Channel are recent features of the European landscape and that Early Man would have been able to walk across from Continental Europe on his hunting expeditions.

The gradual retreat of the ice left the district with a veneer of glacial debris over the lower-lying land, and the earlier soils would have been eroded off the uplands.[1] Drainage would be impaired and lakes would be major features of the landscape. Terminal moraines blocked the Ribble at Long Preston holding back a lake three miles long, and the Wharfe was dammed at Grassington, so melt water flooded Upper Wharfedale and Littondale. Kingsdale above Thornton Force was also drowned. Malham Tarn was then twice its present size, and low-lying mosses like Austwick Moss would have been areas of water. A tarn which formed beneath the scars at Giggleswick was drained in 1863 and at higher levels there would be water masses. The majority have been drained but some can still be seen at Attermire.

The picture of the district must then be one of valleys badly drained and unsuitable for unhindered movement, contrasting markedly with the limestone plateau.

The barren, recently glaciated lands did not suddenly clothe themselves in grass or oak forest. Lichen and the hardier arctic and alpine assemblages slowly established themselves, so that organic soils improved as more warmth and vegetation became available. Most of our knowledge of the ecological history of the district is based on pollen analysis. Pollen grains, though microscopic, are preserved more or less indefinitely in waterlogged and very acid soils and peats. A sample from a core of lake mud or from the blanket of peat on the fellside may well contain fossil pollen carried from the vegetation around that site at some time in the past. A vertical series of samples should give a picture of changes in the ecology and therefore some of the environmental conditions of the district may be envisaged.

The early zones, dated in the North-West to about 10,000 years B.C., show evidence of grasses, sedges, pine, willow and juniper joined by tree birches. This open tundra was inhabited by bear (*Ursus arctos*), horse (*Equus caballus*), reindeer (*Cervus elaphus*) and hare (*Lepus timidus*); these animals were hunted by small groups of people. Hunting parties would have journeyed from Continental Europe, in the first place possibly only in summer, returning to fixed camps for winter.

Archaeologically, this time period is known as the Upper Palaeolithic (The Old Stone Age), but no uniform culture was spread over Western Europe. The people were thinly scattered and the various cultures are named after the type sites, Solutrean after La Solutre in Central France, and Magdalenian after La Madeleine, which is a site a little south west of Lasceaux also in Central France. Some groups used flint or stone weapons but the finds from this area are of bone or antler. The Abbe Breuil considered the cylindrical reindeer horn rods from Victoria Cave to be Magdalenian. To these must be added an example from Kilnsey Cave with a more

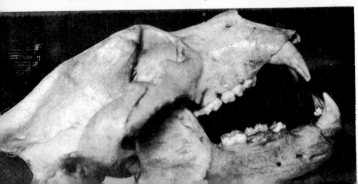

*Left:*
*Cave Bear*
*from*
*Victoria Cave.*

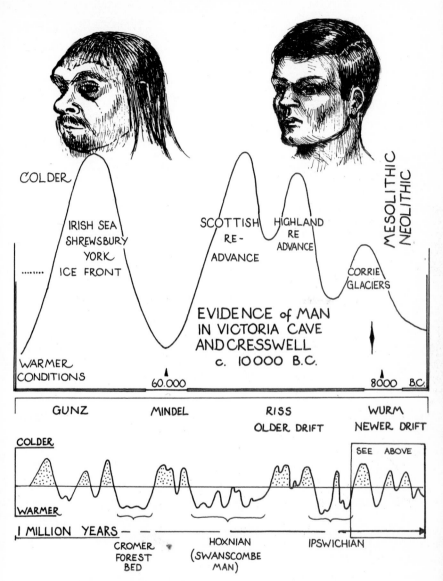

COLDER

IRISH SEA
SHREWSBURY
YORK
ICE FRONT

........

SCOTTISH
RE-
ADVANCE

HIGHLAND
RE
ADVANCE

CORRIE
GLACIERS

MESOLITHIC
NEOLITHIC

EVIDENCE of MAN
IN VICTORIA CAVE
AND CRESSWELL
c. 10000 B.C.

WARMER
CONDITIONS

60.000

8000  B.C.

| GUNZ | MINDEL | RISS | WURM |
|------|--------|------|------|
| | | OLDER DRIFT | NEWER DRIFT |

COLDER

SEE  ABOVE

WARMER

I MILLION YEARS — — —

CROMER
FOREST
BED

HOXNIAN
(SWANSCOMBE
MAN)

IPSWICHIAN

The Pleistocene Ice Age was not one period of cold, but many.
During the most recent, the Newer Drift or Wurm Glacial,
Modern man (Homo Sapiens) appeared. Neanderthal Man
(Homo Neanderthalensis) died out about 40,000 B.C.

19

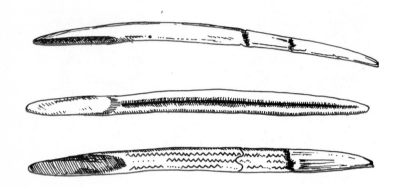

**Fish lance from**

**VICTORIA CAVE,**

**Reconstruction below.**

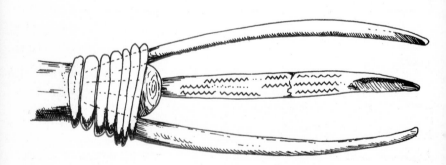

squared section, marked with paired lines faintly scored longitudinally.

A find with a much deeper longitudinal groove, found in 1931 at Victoria Cave, must be either a curved lance head or a fish spear prong and the facet on the broader portion on the inside of the curve, a basal facet needed for hafting. Being curved it cannot be a simple harpoon and it is envisaged as one of perhaps three prongs on a bird lance or fish spear. Zig-zag lines ornamenting the inner face could be a motif associated with water; if this is so then the implement must have been a fish spear. This find is almost identical with some of the German examples from Petersfels,[2] the only apparent difference being that the German examples are straight.

Slowly the birch woodlands were colonized by hazel and later by the broad-leaved deciduous trees. But the climate had not warmed up progressively, for as late as about 8,000 B.C. there was a small glacial advance, the ice being limited to the Scottish Highlands and possibly to upland cirques and valley ends in Northern England. By about 5,000 B.C. Britain was separated from the Continent and the climatic warming-up had reached an optimum, with the British Isles enjoying a climate more like that of Southern Europe today.

In the North-West the Mesolithic period is characterized in some localities by a scatter of small flint blades. The caves have yielded flint and bone finds, possibly the best known being the Azilian harpoon head from Victoria Cave, Settle. This is made of antler and has a rounded base which would have been fixed, possibly by resin, to the harpoon shaft. A line would also have been attached to the head for drawing in the smitten prey.

The number of flints found in the major cave excavation is small; this is hardly surprising when we read that the labourers had dug outside Victoria Cave to a depth of 12 feet when they discovered the Azilian harpoon.[3]

On the surface, flints of Mesolithic - microlithic form have been found at a variety of sites, but the south-facing slopes around Malham Tarn have produced the greatest number. It would appear that the tarn was linked to an expanse of water in what is now Great Close and that this was a favoured fishing spot. In the south-west, on the fells surrounding Catnot Mire (again close to the 1,250 ft. contour), microliths are found on patches of white sand where the peat has been eroded. These are usually chert, which in the Slaidburn district occurs naturally in bands and nodules varying in

*Right:*
*Azilian*
*harpoon.*

thickness from inches to the massive Sykes chert which is 25 ft. thick.[4] Flint on the other hand will have to be imported.

The upland flints, blunted backpoints, batterbacks, microburins and, rarely, thumb scrapers, are smaller than the cave flints, which are usually worked to a point. Patination on them all varies but if we may base cultural connections on the colours of the flints, these appear to be with East Yorkshire and not with the flints of the Lake District-Furness area. Generally speaking flints of the Pennine area belong to the Non-Geometric phase and were considered by Clarke to be probably the earliest in Britain, they were certainly earlier than the Geometric industry of the south of England.[5]

As stated earlier, peat can provide pollen which may be used as a guide in reconstructing the landscape's previous vegetation cover. Professor D. Walker was fortunate at the Stump Cross site near Pateley Bridge in being able to link man with the forest history. Flints were found in situ, and samples taken from the peat showed that deciduous forest, mainly of oak, elm and alder had spread over the district.

1. *There is no evidence to prove that the ice has finally retreated, bearing in mind the time span of the glaciation, over two million years, and the fact that the most recent retreat in the North of England was 20,000 years B.P.*
2. *Garrod, D.—Proc. Prehist. Soc. IV, Plate II (1938).*
3. *Excavation was not trowel and bucket work in 1870. It was done with pick and shovel, the men being paid 1s. 6d. a day.*
4. *Moseley, F.—Proc. Yorkshire Geological Soc. 32, p.290. (1962).*
5. *Clark, J. G. D.—"The Mesolithic Age in Britain" (1932).*
*Two articles concerning the study of fossil pollen are available locally. One, published as an offprint, is "The Stratigraphy and Pollen analysis of Malham Tarn and Tarn Moss," by Prof. and Mrs. Pigott. (Field Studies Vol. 1, No. 1.). The other, "An Introduction to the Ecological History of N.W. England" by Prof. Frank Oldfield is Vol. 3 of "The Changing Scene" (1966).*
*The best introduction to flint tools is a British Museum publication, "Man the Toolmaker," by K. P. Oakley.*

# PALAEOLITHIC CARVINGS

*This probable example of early cave art was found in Victoria Cave.*

# *3. Forest Clearance*

THE most recent part of the Stone Age is known as the Neolithic or New Stone Age, but it must be stressed that this period is not a continuation of the earlier ones and it is unlikely to have developed as the outcome of local Mesolithic traditions. A cultural break occurred, probably in the western parts of Asia, and the spread of farming created possibilities of economic advance for the prehistoric Europeans. The change from a food-gathering to food-producing community can only have taken place where wild animals and plants existed to be domesticated. It can be argued that man did not wisely choose the animals he was to adopt, but goats, sheep, swine and cattle are still pastorally with us; the horse was tamed at a much later date.

At Jericho, and at farms in Iraq, farming communities existed with their flocks and crops of cereals up to about 6,000 BC. Stone and flint tools, including sickles, were used, but there was no pottery. In Greece and the Balkans the earliest agricultural communities are about 1,000 years later and from their mud brick buildings and clay models of houses it seems a short step to pottery figurines and utensils. This may be so in a sun-baked environment, but the production of pottery in the damper zones of Europe necessitated the use of fire and possibly some form of kiln or oven. Penetration of Western Europe via the Danube and the sea routes of the Mediterranean, eventually led to the Neolithic colonization of the British Isles by about the year 3,000 BC.

The immigrant farmers moving into Western Europe cultivated the lighter soils, and in England the Windmill Hill people settled on the chalklands; for although the neighbouring clay vales may have been richer they would have been much more difficult to farm. In West Yorkshire and North Lancashire the limestone scars were wooded but there were some patches of open ground. This has been confirmed by the presence of pollen of the rock rose (*Helianthemum*). The

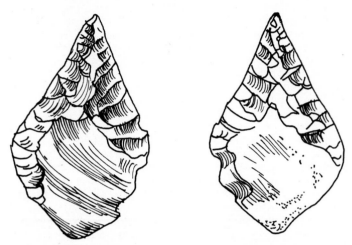

*Neolithic leaf-shaped arrowhead from Catnot, Bowland fells.*

valleys were more thickly forested, and as rainfall seems to have decreased the plateaux and scars would have provided rich organic soils. Pollen diagrams, resulting from work on the peats of North-West England, show changes which cannot be attributed with any certainty to climatic change. The evidence may be much more convincingly interpreted as a response to human activity, especially as most of the evidence for man is through the chance finds of polished stone axes. Hand axes, usually of flint, had been used earlier but the Neolithic axe is usually fabricated from an igneous rock once hafted to a wooden handle.

In the North-West an axe factory has been found on a scree slope south of the Pike of Stickle at the head of Langdale Valley. The grey-green stone is a volcanic tuff. Terry Manby, researching on the Neolithic, drew up a series of trade routes across the north of England from Langdale.[1] His Craven

Route follows the southern edge of the limestone, but traders appear to have carried more than just Cumbrian axes for an axe found in the Ribble at Langcliffe appears to be a basalt example from Tievebulliagh, Antrim; flint examples found on Knowe Fell, at Trenhouse and in Crummackdale show that flint was being imported to the district from the chalk lands of eastern England.

The polished axe is much more efficient than one that has simply been chipped to shape, but flint flakes were still used as scrapers knives and arrowheads. Tranchet and leaf-shaped arrowheads are most beautifully worked but usually they are isolated finds. No camps or settlements are known in the district although some caves and rock shelters have yielded pottery and what could be interpreted as occupation debris. Sherds of coarse bowls, the fabric containing angular bits of quartz and calcite, with "stabbed" or finger nail decoration, have been found with disarticulated bodies in caves.

Sewell Cave yielded six bodies and a burnt skull, and Lesser Kelco four. Excavations at Foxholes in Clapdale and at Elbolton Cave in Wharfedale revealed features interpreted as "sepulchral areas", burials being found in stone walled enclosures against the cave wall. In addition the Foxholes site produced a variety of animal bones including cattle species, (*Bos primigenius and Bos longifrons*), red deer, (*Cerves elaphas*), Roe deer (*Cervus capreolus*), Boar (*Sus scrofa ferus*) and Wolf (*Canis lupus*). They suggest a wooded countryside, but the cattle species must have had clearings for grazing. Did Neolithic man live in caves, or did he only use them as burial sites? The other possibility is that human remains, especially disarticulated bodies, could prove cannibalism.

Hafting axes solid enough to stand hard use in forest clearance appears to have been a problem for in the later Neolithic period axes are perforated and their form changed to axe hammers.

From the evidence of recent peasant communities clearing woodland, the trees do not have to be felled. "Ring barking" will kill the tree and admit more light to the ground. Later the dead trees can be burnt and the wood ash unconsciously used as a fertilizer. Plots cleared in this way would have the ground broken up but not ploughed. Axe hammers may have been used for gardening and so might the smaller edged cushion maces, though the perforation of this later form is small, and the shaft would have to be light; nevertheless they could have been used as hoes. It is possibly worth mentioning that these small maceheads, or hoes, have been found in the upland peats the highest one at 1,400 feet about a mile south of Penyghent summit. Their distribution is not confined to the Pennine area, examples having been found in the Lake District. No serious study of these implements seems to have been made.

Slowly man has lowered the tree line from at least 1,600 feet in the Lake District to its present altitude; at different times forest has made a "come back" on the lowlands. The initial Neolithic attack on the forests probably occurred in a favourable dry and warm period, so that man's activity was exaggerated by the climate and made it more difficult for nature to repair. The wetter period that followed encouraged the development of "raised bogs" on the low lying mosses and "blanket bog" over the Pennine hills.

Burials have already been noted as occurring in various caves and these are the exception rather than the rule, few districts of the British Isles having caves available. Generally Neolithic burials took place in long barrows. These tombs, built of massive stones, can be compared with subterranean rock cut examples from Mediterranean lands. In Britain a variety of forms are found, from a single burial chamber approached along a narrow passage to large gallery graves having pairs of side chambers opposed along the passage. The massively-built chambers and passage are covered by a long mound of earth or stone.

Long barrows, common on the chalk lands of the East Riding, are rare in the Pennines, and when they are found they appear to be degenerate types. Giant's Grave, at the head of Penyghent Gill, was first mentioned by Dr. Whitaker in 1812. It is clear that skeletons were found in stone cists but no other finds are mentioned.[2] A little digging was done at the eastern end in 1936 and from this and the surface evidence W. Bennett suggests that the site was a passage grave or a multiple cist burial. The stone cairn is now badly eroded but the large limestone slabs that make up the cist sides are easily seen. There may have been an entrance in a flat facade at the western end, though normally these forms have their entrances in the south-east.

In Westmorland there is evidence of another long barrow situated on Rayseat Pike near Crosby Ravensworth and the skeletal fragments were found in cremation trenches. This fact does make dating difficult, as cremation is usually taken as evidence of a Bronze Age date. Both the barrows are, in fact, cairns composed of stones and not earth, and it appears that the Rayseat Pike example is a stray from Yorkshire.

A more modest and certainly more unique burial was the one located on South House Moor, north east of Simon Fell, where a female skeleton was found. Sir Arthur Keith describes the bones as belonging to "a very short woman not more than 4ft. 10ins, probably 35 to 40 years old and very feminine; that is to say she had kept many of her girlish features: her skull is only 3 to 4 millimetres thick and there were no ridges over the root of her nose." The body had been placed in a gryke (a solution-widened crack) of the limestone pavement and was covered with a slab. With the body was a large polished Langdale stone axe head. Perhaps women were equally responsible with men for forest clearance, whatever their appearance.

The caves were used by Neolithic folk, and while axes and graves of the same date are found there is no evidence in this district to indicate if the people led a settled life or moved about the country. But it is clear that a pastoral farmer is more settled than a Palaeolithic hunter, and the camps of the chalklands, with their stockpounds and large quantities of bones from animals slaughtered in autumn, show that it is likely that people were settling permanently on the better lands.

Thick coarse pottery was being made into fairly large bowls decorated with stabbed lines or lines of dots, some potters using a broken bird bone to incise the clay,[4] others employing their fingertips or finger nails. The thick pots are rather porous, grog (crushed stone), being added to the clay to give the pot strength when it was in a plastic state, Sometimes fragments of stone from the grog, cut into microscope sections, can be identified and the source located. It is no wonder that a popular British Museum booklet is called *The Neolithic Revolution*, for greater changes had taken place during that period.

1. *Manby, T. G.*—*"Transactions of the Cumberland and Westmorland Antiquarian Society," Vol. LXV, p*1. (1965).
2. *Whitaker, T. D.*—*"History of Craven"* (1812).

ALL-OVER-CORD DECORATED
BEAKER FROM GRASSINGTON
*The beaker, which is seven inches high,
can be seen in The Craven Museum, Skipton.*

29

**A COMB-DECORATED BEAKER**
*An example of Clarke's southern British beaker group, excavated by Mr. W. Holgate at Rectory Allotment, Earby. The height of this beaker is five and a-half inches; it is now in the Craven Museum, Skipton.*

# 4. The Bronze Age Metalworkers

WHILE the Neolithic farmers with their stone tools were establishing a farming way of life in Britain, Egypt and Mesopotamia had advanced technologically to become complex, literate metalworking civilizations. Techniques used in firing pottery in kilns were probably adapted to produce metals. Copper does occur naturally and can be cold hammered into shape but this does not imply a knowledge of smelting, so early evidence for copper working in Persia can be ignored. Advances stemmed from the Eastern Mediterranean region, by 2500 B.C. there were copper-working colonies in Southern Spain and Southern Portugal linked by archaeological finds of pottery with cultures from the shores of the Aegean sea.

How did new traditions spread through more backward communities? The axe traders of the previous chapter, now trading with bronzes, would not convert the ignorant. A class of itinerant smiths who carried ingots of metal with them, or knew the ore sources, seems more likely. This assumes a good deal of knowledge, for some areas of Europe rich in archaeological bronze goods have no local ores. Similarly, in Britain, copper is found mainly in the upland areas of Cornwall, North Wales—especially Anglesey—and Ireland. Did prospectors search the country and set up trade in ingots? Boats were being used to cross to Ireland, and doubtless dug-out canoes carried goods down rivers.

It seems likely that the copper-working colonists in southern Iberia were wiped out by the native inhabitants of the area who, having acquired the knowledge of copper-working, proceeded to spread the knowledge over the greater part of Europe. These people were makers of Bell-Beaker pottery and the Beaker ceramics, relatively fine buff ware with horizontal zones of impressed decoration in marked contrast with the earlier Neolithic bowls.

The beakers are often associated, with wrist guards of bone or stone and fine tang and barbed flint arrowheads, with burials under a barrow or tumulus. Graves, which were no

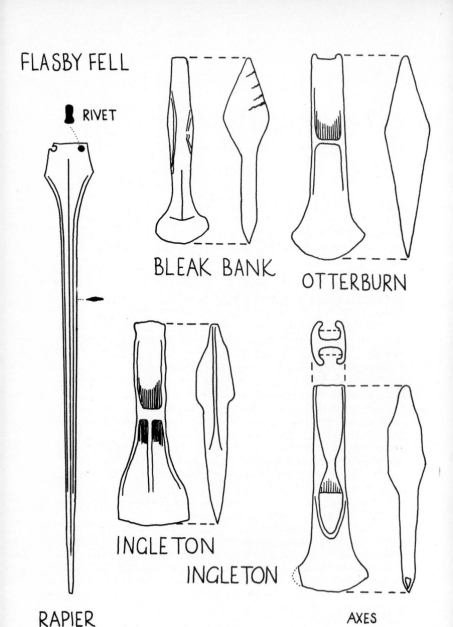

FLASBY FELL

RIVET

BLEAK BANK

OTTERBURN

INGLETON

INGLETON

RAPIER

AXES

BRONZE AXES AND
A RAPIER

32

longer communal forms but many barrows, each covering a single grave, can be found together at localities that must have been religious cemetery sites. The men were therefore archers, and the high quality of goods sometimes found in graves could suggest a warrior aristocracy. Certainly they were not solely exploiting copper ores but other non ferrous material, including gold. The new technology was carried along Atlantic coast sea routes to Brittany, the Low Countries and possibly Britain.

Immigration seems to have been across the North Sea from the neighbourhood of the Rhine Estuary to the east coast of England, with the result that few beakers have been found in the Pennine area of Lancashire compared with the very numerous finds from the chalk and limestone wolds of the East and North Ridings. Study has been made of the pottery shapes and of the type of decoration together with the associated finds. Computers are speeding up research in this field and the C14 (radio carbon dating method) will give more accurate dates.

The Beaker period was fairly brief, possibly only 200 years, and Lancashire has yielded fragmentary evidence for only three beakers. The best preserved example may have been found at Woolston, near Warrington but there is some doubt about it. The base of another to be seen in Keighley Museum, is said to have been found near Burnley. One sherd has definitely been found in Dog Hole Cave, near Carnforth. Pottery finds increase in the east, with the Yorkshire Wolds and Northumberland being particularly well blessed. It is clear that immigrants from Continental Europe were landing along the east coast.

The limestone hills of Craven and Furness have yielded beaker sherds, the finest being a Cord-zoned example found at Grassington. Recently an excavation near Earby, south of Skipton, produced a fine selection of pottery types, the earliest being a long necked beaker with incised decoration. (The potter seems to have used a comb for applying the patterns of chevrons around the base and bands and diamonds around the neck). A jet pulley lay with the beaker, implying links with North Yorkshire as most jet occurs in the Whitby neighbourhood. Here a number of burials had taken place beneath the same large stone cairn and the pottery associated with them is Bronze Age. The Earby finds are now in the Craven Museum at Skipton.

Beaker graves sometimes contain archer's equipment, and in particular bone or stone wrist guards. These give way to a new assemblage of weapons, usually the axe and dagger The "new" weapons cast in bronze have their prototypes in. central Europe, just north of the Alps, and we can again see evidence for long distance trade and travel.

Examples of flat axes and rivetted daggers in the early Bronze Age were as rare as beakers in the North-West but finds from later dates gradually increase in number, as more people moved into the district. Burial rituals changed slightly in that the corpse was no longer interred in a crouched position but cremated, and the ashes and bone fragments placed in a cinerary urn. The ashes were accompanied by the dead persons weapons, sometimes jewellery and accessory cups, under the burial mound.

A mound on Lingber Hill, near Hellifield, was opened in 1889 and can be taken as an example. Here two urns were found, and each was covered by a gritstone slab. The larger urn was 12 ins. high and contained a small bronze blade, which could be either a tanged and riveted dagger or a razor, a 3 inch sharp bone needle and an unidentifiable but riveted piece of metal. The smaller urn, which would have stood about 10 ins. high had it not been badly broken, was on top of fragments of a third vessel which contained calcined bones and an accessory cup.

A much rarer burial was discovered by Dr. W. J. Varley when he excavated in Bleasdale, on the southern flanks of the Bowland Fells. He found the remains of a timber circle, a wood henge with a single interment placed in it.[1] This burial was also accompanied by urns and an accessory cup. The Bleasdale accessory cup is one of a small group that have been found in or close to Ribblesdale. They are similar in shape and much larger than the normal English form. The cup from Waddington (now in Clitheroe Museum), is almost 7 ins. in diameter, while the one from Earby is over $5\frac{1}{2}$ inches. Accessory cups found further north are smaller but they are of the same fine quality ceramic. This pink, or buff ware must be linked with the flood vessel forms of the northern Irish Sea zone. They are in no way similar to cups found in the East or North Ridings, where the truncated cone (trunconic) shape is common but they do resemble pots found in Northern Ireland and South-West Scotland.

It seems sensible that trade across the Irish Sea should be from the white limestone headlands around the northern part of Morecambe Bay. The landforms would certainly aid navigation and, crossing close to the Isle of Man, would be much shorter than any attempt from the mouth of the Ribble. Sir

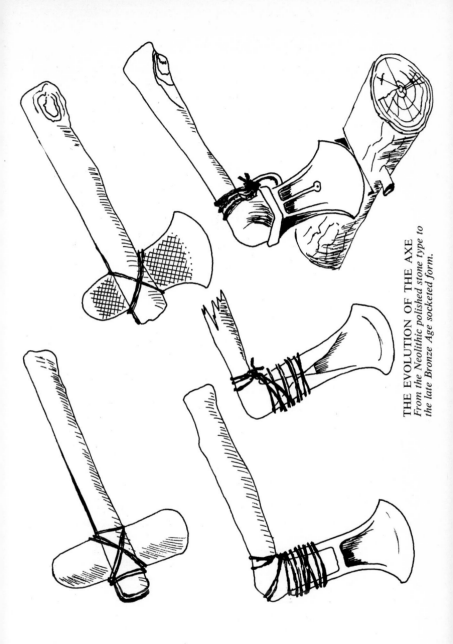

THE EVOLUTION OF THE AXE
*From the Neolithic polished stone type to the late Bronze Age socketed form.*

Cyril Fox considered the Ribble and Aire valleys to be a major trans-Pennine routeway during the Bronze Age. Now it appears as though the Hodder and Calder valleys were also used. Whalley and Skipton have as long a traffic history as anywhere in the north, but downstream from Whalley the

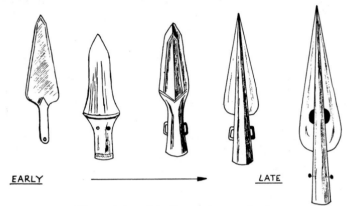

EARLY ⟶ LATE

*The evolution of the Bronze Age spearhead.*

peat mosses and boulder clay-covered areas of the Lancashire Plain and the Fylde were ignored.

Individual finds and hoards of the Bronze Age exist in most museums, and text books set out the evolution of the types diagramatically.[2] The finding of implements does not imply that bronzes were made locally, though it it likely that itinerant smiths fabricated wares from scrap metal, wherever the demand arose, and the evolution of new forms was again not local but common over the greater part of Britain.

Today uplands are being used more frequently for water storage by the large industrial towns, and it was during one of the many pipe-laying operations that in 1966 a small hoard of metalwork was found. in Portfield Camp, Whalley, the find consisted of two bronze socketed axes, a bronze tanged knife, a bronze gouge and three other unidentifiable pieces of bronze, possibly scrap, together with a gold bracelet and a gold tress ring. The tress ring has been considered by Dr. Ian Longworth to be an Irish import but the form of the bracelet he thinks is not Irish. Yet it is likely that the gold itself came from that country and was made for the north British market.[3]

A more unusual find, from a trenching operation at Ingleton, was a large disc-headed pin with a perforation in the pin shaft

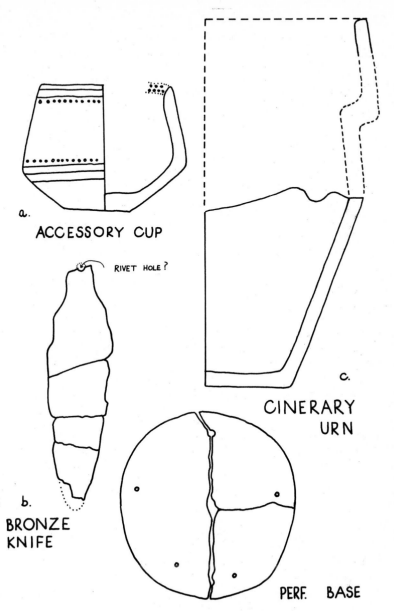

a.
ACCESSORY CUP

RIVET HOLE?

b.
BRONZE
KNIFE

c.
CINERARY
URN

PERF. BASE

*Finds from the Bronze Age burial mound on Lingber Hill, Hellifield. The urn stood about 10 ins. high and the accessory cup 2 ins. high.*

37

hidden beneath a diamond shaped plate. Almost 6 ins. long, it was either a native attempt to copy an un-familiar object, or an advance on simpler pin forms from the south of England. Even so this type of pin is very rare in England and stems from objects of North European origin. Culturally it can be linked with Denmark, North Germany and even Bohemia, and dates from the Late Bronze Age, possibly about 700 B.C.

The increased number of people in Britain could not all have been leading contented lives at this time for the dagger had evolved into the rapier; one was found on Flasby Fell near Skipton. It was of a type common to the London area, $19\frac{1}{2}$ins. long, with two rivets to hold on the handle that is now missing. Every local museum has examples of the small socketed axe, and while the casting technique of manufacture is interesting their site spots are also noteworthy. Axes found on Ingleborough and near Rathmell were deep in peat, and from the peat comes the evidence of a deteriorating climate. The drier Bronze Age gave way to more normal British weather, and perhaps during the Bronze Age stout weatherproof dwellings were not as essential as they were to natives of the suceeding period. Few local settlements have been dated conclusively, yet people who built monuments for the dead, whether in wood or stone, had the ability to house themselves and probably their breeding stock.

From other parts of Britain comes evidence of ploughing and textile manufacture, good quality woollens and worsteds having been found woven in a variety of patterns and colours. The best-preserved garments again come from depths in peat mosses, but peat cutting locally has lapsed and the supply of finds has been interrupted. In 1846 a body was found by peat cutters about 10 ins. down in the peat of Austwick Moss. Shoes located nearby had originally had nails in the soles in a figure of eight pattern, so presumably the person belonged to the Iron Age.

1. *Varley, W. J.—"The Bleasdale Circle", Antiquaries Journal, Vol. XVIII* 154-225. (1938).
2. *Grimes, W. F.—"The Prehistory of Wales," pp.65-69, (1951).*
3. *Longworth, I. H.—"Bronze Age Hoard from Portfield Camp, Whalley,"* Brit. Museum Quarterly, Vol. XXXII, No. 1.
   The best summary of Bronze Age burial and burial mounds is possibly "The Bronze Age Round Barrow in Britain", by P. Ashbee (1960).

# 5. The Celtic and Roman Iron Age

THE turmoil on the Continent during the latter part of what was here the Late Bronze Age can be read elsewhere.[1] Cultural and material changes stem back to the break-up of the Hittite Empire, when techniques of iron-working spread into eastern Europe. The Hallstatt horsemen in Continental Europe used iron in their long swords during the seventh century B.C. In East Yorkshire they appeared later and their graves were characterized by the fact that the warriors were sometimes buried with a wagon, or cart and horse trappings which are found to date from as late as the Second century B.C.

This chapter is devoted to the art of these Celtic people. Fundamentally what remains for us in the north of England is a remarkable suite of metalwork. In the North, the smiths carried on their trade after the Roman Conquest, from when it becomes possible to date finds from their association, if they were associated, with Roman pottery and coins. Celtic traditions obviously exist today in the upland areas of the north and west of the British Isles and for that matter in the valleys, but there they are less easily discerned.

The introduction of wrought iron (remembering the fact that tempering and steel-making were later, almost recent, techniques), did not bring an end to bronze work. Bronze casting and enamelling, together with a superb understanding of line, make this period for me the high water mark of British art. This is a personal opinion and many will disagree; nevertheless the barbarians have for too long been considered as skin clad beings hiding in their caves and rude houses.

There is little Craven evidence of Iron Age finds prior to the coming of the Romans, yet the increase in population must have continued throughout the Late Bronze Age and into the Iron Age. A number of irregular stone-walled enclosures on Malham Moor, and elsewhere on the limestone plateau, appear to be stock pounds. They lie at about the same altitude as the better-defined Romano British settlements but are not associated with huts or hut groups. These could be earlier than the First century and would suggest some pastoralism in the area.

The ultimate Bronze population did not evolve new techniques, though lead may have replaced tin in the bronze of the Late Bronze Age. The people appear to have been submerged beneath new and more vigorous communities. Material wealth changed remarkably during the first three centuries A.D., and from the settlement evidence (to be discussed in the next chapter) the population increased greatly. Bronze remained the most common surviving metal, but silver and gold were also used. Iron was the principal metal, being used for edged cutting tools, from swords to small knives and shears, but it is seldom preserved. Bronze items were decorated with enamel, coral studs and fine engraving.

Many authors have written about individual and groups of metal objects, some of which were single chance finds picked up on the surface or in ploughing or drainage schemes. But the majority were found in the caves and are now in various museum collections. Settle has many of these, but some metal objects excavated from caves in King's Scar in 1848 and from Dowkerbottom Cave, near Kilnsey in 1857 are in the British Museum.

The Ingleton Mirror Handle (actually found at Coldcotes), was dated by Sir Cyril Fox to about 40 A.D. With a length of 6½ ins. it is a bronze type of handle with a ring at both ends. The upper ring has two cows heads symmetrically positt ioned as integral parts of the mirror grip, and they show that the missing mirror would have been kidney shaped, not circular. Another mirror handle found in Spider Cave, Settle, appears to be similar but the upper ring is missing. It is not as fine an example and is probably later than the Ingleton find.

*Left: The Ingleton Mirror Handle. (British Museum).*

40

**BRONZE
DRAGONESQUE
BROOCHES**

*Above:
From Attermire.*

*Left:
Enamelled brooch
from Victoria
Cave.*

41

The most common bronze objects found in the cave excavations were the fibulae or brooches. The bronze casting and enamelling of the Brigantian smiths was superb. (Brigantia was the district north of the Rivers Mersey and Trent extending as far as the Scottish borders, possibly even into the Scottish foothills of Dumfriesshire. It was said by Tacitus the Roman author to be "the most populous state in the whole province"). R. G. Collingwood classified the Romano-British brooches according to type in 1930 and while the book has recently been republished his classification remains.[2]

First century brooches are rare but in the first half of the Second century two forms of brooch were quite common. This increase in production of brooches due to the more settled conditions that followed the initial conquest of the North of England and the establishment of Hadrian's Wall. The "S" shaped brooch, which evolved into the Dragonesque form is prominent in collections. R. W. Feachem has shown that these brooches were popular in the North and in southern Scotland; they have been found at Traprain Law, the Lothian hillfort; Corbridge, Northumberland, and in the Settle caves. All local examples have been cast in bronze and later decorated, the find from Attermire Cave having punched lines breaking the flowing outline and the leaf-like detail above the "eye" is almost identical to that of the Victoria Cave brooch which is enamelled.

The champleve enamelling technique was used on this and many other bronze brooches. A design was gouged out of the metal or cast on the blank of the brooch during the initial process. The enamel which was a powdered mixture of flint or sand, containing metallic oxides, was placed on the red hot metal in the areas of the brooch to be coloured. A high tempperature was necessary to melt the powder and a sharp burr edge had to be present to hold in the molten enamel. Obviously specialized tools, tweezers and measures would be needed and some of these have been found. Clay moulds, slag metal and furnaces have also been discovered.

The other fibula common in the north of England on most Roman and Romano-British sites is the trumpet type. The acanthus which decorates the waist of the brooch has been borrowed from classical sources. Artistic qualities were very high and we can see that the Celtic bronze-smith was able to continue his craft after the Roman conquest of the North for at least a few generations.It is conceivable that the Romans encouraged the craftsmen during the period when the dragonesque and trumpet brooches were being made. The increasing

ROMANO-
BRITISH
BROOCHES:

*Right: Bronze dish
brooch, one and a-half
inches in diameter.
Below: Two aspects of a
silver trumpet-headed fibula.*

use of coins made marketing easier and examples of these bronzes have been found in Central Europe. It is not yet known whether bi-products of Roman lead mining provided a supply of raw materials for the Celtic smiths but a few brooches were worked in silver.

Another type of brooch found in considerable numbers is the disc brooch bearing abstract patterns in relief. The best examples show a balanced, three part, triscelis trumpet scroll design. So similar is the character of these discs that they could have come from one centre of manufacture and again they date to the first part of the Second century. From the evidence of the brooches, trade and communications with the rest of the Northern Province had developed and expanded considerably during the century.

The defeat of the Brigantes at Stanwick near Catterick in the year 74 A.D. was a major blow, but in the west living conditions may have improved. Our district is ringed by forts founded during the Agricolan period at Ribchester, Elslack, Ilkley, Bainbridge and Lancaster, and although Hadrian had forces withdrawn from 120 garrisons in the Pennine area the forts in the west remained manned. In about 150 A.D. an uprising occurred in the Western Pennines and Roman reinforcements had to be brought from the Continent. Most of the early Agricolan forts had been turf and timber constructions and they were sacked. Bainbridge fort was rebuilt in stone as early as as 158 A.D. but was possibly sacked again in 197 A.D. The forts at Elslack and Ilkley were rebuilt after 210 A.D. Finds of occasional pieces of Scottish horse riding fittings could prove that the Caledonian hordes, who swept over Hadrian's Wall in 197 A.D., reached as far south as Giggleswick; otherwise a series of revolts occured in the district throughout the second half of the Second century.

The first century fibulae were left by immigrants moving into the thinly populated Dales valleys, but second century finds are locally made. Articles of bronze, lead, silver and of course, iron are found. Ingots or "pigs" of lead (weighing 155 lbs and 156 lbs respectively) were discovered on Hayshaw Bank near Pateley Bridge, and dated to the year 81 A.D. Another found on Greenhow Hill east of Grassington bore the name of the Emperor Trajan, who died in 117 A.D. It is clear then, that lead was mined in the Grassington district. The mineral veins extended as far west as the scars in which Attermire and Victoria Caves are found. Ore has been removed by surface working and Dr. Raistrick pointed out that the good mineral ore is associated with the shallowest workings and no ex-

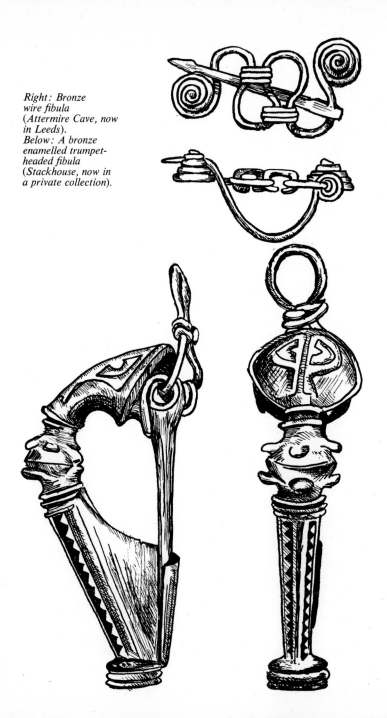

*Right: Bronze wire fibula (Attermire Cave, now in Leeds).*
*Below: A bronze enamelled trumpet-headed fibula (Stackhouse, now in a private collection).*

tensive surface mining has been continued successfully by
deep shafts.

Common minerals in the area include galena (lead sulphide),
anglesite (lead sulphate), calamine (now called smithsonite-
zinc carbonate), malachite and azurite (both copper carbonates), barytes, fluorspar. quartz and calcite. It is evident that
some mineral sulphide ores, exposed at the surface to weather-
ing, have become carbonates; these would have been worked
in prehistoric times, as metals can be produced directly from
the ores. Malachite, for instance, can be smelted at a temperature of 700°—800° C., a temperature that could be reached
using wood fuel and a very simple furnace. The pottery produced at that time would have needed about the same firing
conditions. Zinc melts at 420° C. and there is no reason why
copper and zinc carbonate ores could not have been smelted
together to produce a metal that is, in fact, brass. No analyses
are available at present to show if what have been considered
to be bronzes are in fact brass.

An excavation at Victoria Camp, on the limestone top above
Victoria Cave, revealed an elongated bowl lined with clay and
containing almost a hundredweight of barytes. The barytes
was impure and contained a good deal of malachite and some

*Below: Two halves of a clay mould for a bronze dress-fastener (from
Traprain Law, Scotland). Nat. Mus. of Antiq., Edinburgh.*

haematite (iron oxide); slag and charcoal were also found. The adjacent circular huts yielded no closely dateable finds, but in one hut wall more barytes was found. Certainly the huts are Romano-British, matching other excavated examples. This settlement, situated at an altitude of 1500 ft. on a waterless plateau, is not a defensive hilltop camp, but there must have been good reason for people to have lived there. The close proximity of the mineral ores has outweighed all other considerations. A small lens-shaped ingot $2\frac{1}{2}$ ins. in diameter was found in either Victoria Cave or Dowkerbottom and is now in the British Museum. This is close to the average size of Roman and Romano—British metallurgical crucibles from the north of England.

Lead spindle whorls are not uncommon finds and are usually decorated with zig-zag lines running around the upper and lower surfaces. This same pattern is found on the front of the cast lead figure from Giggleswick. Although the lady appears to be dressed in a full length skirt there is no reason to think that this proves a recent date. Iron Age burials in the Danish bogs have been found clothed in dresses of similar length woven in wool and associated with shawls and skin capes. Like the Danish bodies, the small figurine could well be a votive offering, given to one of the Celtic gods in return for a

*Below: Cast lead figurine from Bank Well, Giggleswick.*

good harvest or possibly a good supply of lead ore. The wells at Giggleswick, especially the Ebbing and Flowing Well, would be considered entrances to the underworld and suitable sites for making offerings.

Conditions in the caves and on the uplands have not favoured the preservation of ironwork, but knives and domestic items like nails, hooks and keys have been found in most caves. A fine sword in its scabbard was found on Flasby Fell, between Gargrave and Skipton, while the example found in Sewell Cave, Settle, is a Roman gladius. The first find was a long slashing type of weapon, the other a short strong form, better used for in-fighting. The arrival of chariots and wagons in East Yorkshire in 500 B.C. and the chariot burials of the Arras district, show how slowly the cultural changes occurred in the upland Pennine areas. Found with the Romano-British bronzes in Attermire Cave are wheel tyres, nave hoops, lynch pin and other chariot fragments. Certainly the vehicle was not "garaged" there, for the cave mouth is about 20 feet above the top of a steep scree slope in a cliff face. The chariot must have been dismantled and carried up in pieces and it is very likely it marks the burial spot of some warrior. The whole collections of fine enamelled bronzes, silver and gilded objects show the caves, like the springs, were religious sites. They were probably sealed after use and there could well be examples that pot-holers will find as they seek exits from the underground systems.

Two large Fourth century brooches, again from Attermire Cave, are both of gold on bronze; they resemble cross-bows in shape and the larger brooch has dolphins decorating the shoulders. Two centuries had passed since the disappearance of the Mediterranean sea dragon of the enamelled dragonesque brooches. The Fourth century craftsman was no longer able to conjure up the plastic forms and it is clear that the standards of work deteriorated during the Roman occupation. A large bronze cauldron found in Crummackdale, north of Austwick, is considered by Professor Hawkes as evidence of continued metalworking by local smiths after the period of unrest.[3] Recently B. R. Hartley, excavating at Bainbridge, found a metalworking area inside the fort. The *principia* was not re-built after being burned down in about 367 AD but seems to have been used as a workshop. Were the native smiths con-scripted into the army? It would have been a sensible way of disarming the belligerent Brigantes.

A number of objects, manufactured from bone or horn were also found in the caves. The most common finds in the

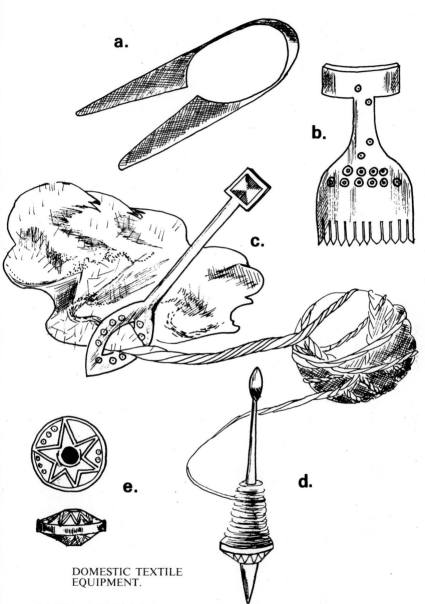

**a.**

**b.**

**c.**

**d.**

**e.**

DOMESTIC TEXTILE
EQUIPMENT.

(*a*) *Clippers.* (*b*) *Comb for removing seeds, burrs and short fibres.* (*c*) *Drawing to produce a rope or sliver.* (*d*) *Spinning.* (*e*) *Spindle whorls. Dyes would be produced from vegetable and mineral sources.*

upland areas of Britain were spoon-shaped, first mentioned and drawn by Boyd Dawkins and described as spoon shaped brooches. While admitting that these objects are beautifully carved and carefully decorated, it's difficult to imagine them pinning together garments of clothing. The style of decoration, single and concentric circles and incised straight lines, is also found on the bone combs and it is most likely that the bone finds were associated in use, as well as being found together archaeologically. Combs are generally accepted as utensils used in the domestic textile industry together with spindles, spindle whorls and needles. Cliffe Castle Museum at Keighley has a display of bone and horn "diz" or discs—items used in the West Riding woollen mills to make up a rope or sliver of wool after it had been combed. The discs were held in the hand between the index finger and the thumb and a rope of wool was drawn through. Like the "spoons" none of the discs is flat, the shape of the bone or horn being utilized to fit the hand. It has been suggested that the spoon-shaped items had exactly the same use as the bone discs.

Iron shears were used for removing wool from the sheep; combed wool with its fibres roughly parallel was drawn through the spoon and twisted. By drawing and twisting a much stronger thread would be produced. The lens and star shaped holes were adaptations in spoon design to make twisting easier; the drawing of the wool through the spoon would certainly aid the final spinning process and a better quality thread would result. High quality twist would be needed as warp on the vertical looms and more would be needed to produce worsted. Bone spindles have been found and it is

*Below: A decorated bone comb from a Settle cave.*

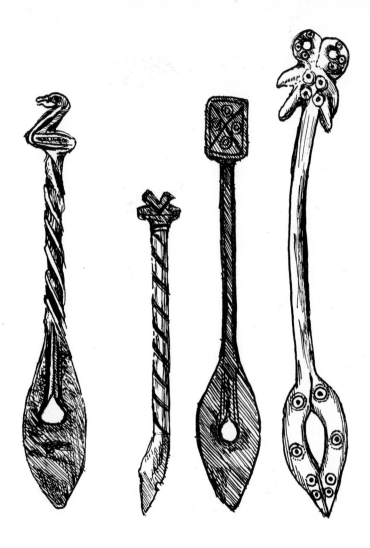

**BONE SPOONS FROM THE CAVES**

*Notice the varied perforations.*
*The decoration is purely Celtic with no borrowing*
*from classical sources.*

likely that wooden ones were also used. To help the action of the spindles, discs were pushed on to the rod; these are called spindle whorls. A variety of these have been found; some made of trimmed pottery others cast in lead, and numerous bone ones. Weaving followed the spinning, and evidence of this process is the loom weights, and the combs used for tightening the weft. The wool would be washed after the spinning and weaving processes, as the grease would help the wool workers, but if plaid cloth of different coloured wools was being woven, then the woollen yarns must have been washed before they were dyed.

It is clear that the West Riding has a very long tradition of wool working and it could be that processes in use during the Romano-British period, on native sites, were forgotten until the domestic woollen industry again became widespread at the beginning of the Industrial Revolution.

1. *Piggott, S.—"Ancient Europe"* (1965).
2. *Collingwood, R. G.—"The Archaeology of Roman Britain"* (1930). *Now reprinted, edited by I. A. Richmond* (1969).
3. *Hawkes, C. C.—"Late Bronze Age-R.B. Cauldrons and Buckets," in "Aspects of Archaeology in Britain and Beyond," Ed. Grimes, W. F.* (1951).

# 6. Celts and Romans —
# The Field Evidence

VISITORS to the Dales will prefer to tour enjoying scenery which at first appears unchanging yet is a record of man's changing use of the land. Much evidence of the Brigantian people and their Roman conquerors is to be found in this area, so field evidence will be emphasised in this chapter.

Other limestone areas in the north-west extend from Kirkby Lonsdale into Furness and along the south-western side of the Eden Valley from Kirkby Stephen.

The chance that hill forts or Roman camps have survived is possibly greater in a pastoral area of sparse population than in the more crowded urban areas which are subject to increasing disturbance yet we have comparatively little information about settlement in the upland areas. Isolation preserved the sites and also limits the number of visiting students; erosion continues, and when sites are excavated the number of finds is low and disappointing. Acid soil rapidly destroys all iron objects, and the poor quality native pottery rarely survives.

The foundations of hut walls and the field systems, together with the situation of the settlement at a spring point or on a hill top, yield information about life almost 2,000 years ago. No native written records are available earlier than the Sixth century AD, but some Roman works do exist and in Ireland, which was not conquered by the Romans, the Iron Age life continued unaltered for centuries; a study here helps us to consider social problems of the times.

From the initial occupation of the limestone areas in the north by the Neolithic people to the expansion on to the grit moors during the Bronze Age, population and the area of land being used slowly increased. A worsening of climatic conditions must have made most upland areas inhospitable. The peat spread and thickened over the fells, in places covering cairns and burials of Bronze Age date. It is not necessary to have a microscope to examine the vegetation in peat, for wood is well preserved and walls along the top of most high fells cross sections, exposing birch boughs and other recognisable

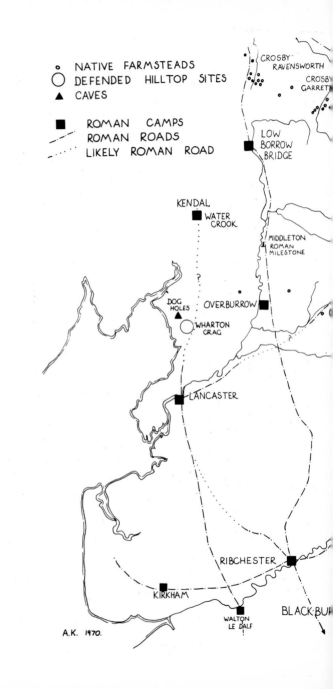

NATIVE FARMSTEADS
DEFENDED HILLTOP SITES
CAVES

ROMAN CAMPS
ROMAN ROADS
LIKELY ROMAN ROAD

CROSBY RAVENSWORTH

CROSBY GARRETT

LOW BORROW BRIDGE

KENDAL
WATER CROOK

MIDDLETON ROMAN MILESTONE

DOG HOLES
OVERBURROW

WHARTON CRAG

LANCASTER

RIBCHESTER

KIRKHAM

WALTON LE DALE

BLACKBURN

A.K. 1970.

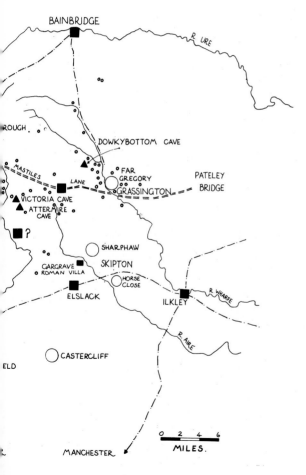

BROUGH

STANWICK

# CELTS AND ROMANS

BAINBRIDGE

R. URE

ROUGH

DOWKYBOTTOM CAVE

MASTILES

LANE

FAR
GREGORY

GRASSINGTON

PATELEY
BRIDGE

VICTORIA CAVE

ATTERMIRE
CAVE

?

SHARPHAW

SKIPTON

GARGRAVE
ROMAN VILLA

HORSE
CLOSE

ELSLACK

ILKLEY

R. WHARFE

R. AIRE

ELD

CASTERCLIFF

MANCHESTER

0  2  4  6
MILES.

plant remains. (It was recently possible for instance, to collect handfuls of hazel nuts on the spoil tips of excavator trenches at Ribchester, where plant remains were preserved by being waterlogged).

For a second time man seems to have appreciated the limestone areas, for in this area most of the evidence for Celtic farming is to be found. The terraces were possibly better drained and the organic soils sweeter than in other districts, so investigation can be concentrated north of the South Craven Fault. Movement on this fault face is responsible for the escarpment that runs south-eastward from the neighbourhood of Ingleton to Settle and on to Skipton.

It is best seen in a journey up Buckhaw Brow from Giggleswick to the north-west, along the main road, the limestone to the north of the road contrast with the millstone grit series on the other side of the road. The road engineers have linked up a series of hamlets mostly situated where springs flow out at the base of the limestone scar on contacting the gritstone. The top of the limestone dips gently northwards and so vanishes beneath the Yoredale Series. In the east, near Grassington, the limestone again disappears beneath the younger rocks of the millstone grit moors. A limestone inlier occurs in Wensleydale and in the tributary valleys the River Bain and also Bishopdale.

*Below: A print from a colour transparency of the limestone hills to the North of Settle, under snow.*

*The valley side between Langcliffe and Stainforth, North Ribblesdale long fields with lynchets (medieval); small squared examples (earlier).*

Other limestone areas in the north-west extend from Kirby Lonsdale into Furness and along the south-western side of the Eden Valley from Kirby Stephen.

This suggests a considerable area available for settlement, but rarely is the limestone plateau very wide and glacial drift buries large areas. Compare the eastern side of the Ribble Valley above Horton with the western side. The search can be limited by careful mapwork. Once the "classic" sites have been visited at High Close, Grassington; below the Cove at Malham; on the terraces south of Ribblehead or at Ewe Close in Westmorland, other limits will suggest themselves to the student.

Seldom are Celtic field systems found on the valley floor; and on the sides 1,200 feet is about the upper limit, though camps are found above 1,500 feet O.D. at Victoria, above Victoria Cave and on Malham Moor above Middle House. It will be easy to find the long strip lynchets of the later medieval ploughmen, and areas, sometimes along the present parish boundaries, show up as pastoral areas of the parishes. e.g.

on the south-facing slopes between Clapham and Austwick, here Celtic fields can be seen. Being square to rectangular in shape, with grass-covered banks or rubble walls separating them, they contrast with the long ribbon-like "furlongs" of the medieval period, but both were used for growing cereal crops. By ploughing along the contour, and by leaving baulks of un-ploughed land between individual holdings, farmers brought lynchets into being. No group of villagers decided to terrace the hillside to make ploughing easier, and stones visible in the steep faces of the lynchets were most likely placed there out of the way of the plough.

In small patchwork groups of enclosed square fields, which are called Celtic fields, few individual fields cover an acre of land. Many are garden-size plots and it is clear that heavy ploughs and teams of draught animals were not used. Small wooden ploughs or ards were more probably used, pulled by a team of two small cows, or the plots could have been cultiva-ted by hoe. Having used the term "acre," before the metric "hectare" takes over, it is possibly worth mentioning that an acre was a furlong by a chain, the first measurement being the distance the team of oxen could plough without discom-fort, a furrow long; during a day's work they should have turned over land a chain wide. On heavy soils progress would be slow, and an acre would have been smaller than on light soils where the plough teams could work more briskly. The area of Celtic fields beneath Malham Cove, already mentioned, is an interesting series, some of the Celtic divisions having been removed or ploughed out during the later period, pro-ducing some long fields running up and down the valley side. Settlements are usually found by spotting the fields from a distance: the best time is late on a summer evening, or in winter when the low angle of the sun throws wide shadows. A thin fall of snow may be melted on the southern side of a bank, again drawing attention to irregularities not previously seen. Among the fields, or tucked in the lee of a limestone terrace on one edge of the fields, there must be some house foundations; the entrances to the Neolithic burial chambers are often in the south-east and the doorways of the circular houses often open in that direction.

It would also be wrong to think that the house foundations are all circular, but it does appear that this is the earliest form, followed by the rectangular variety; there are many sites with both forms. The rectangular form was more common on the Continent, being built in timber, and our stone forms may have evolved from earlier timber examples. Dr. George Jobey, working in Northumberland and Durham, has been unable to date any circular stone foundations to the pre-Roman era and evidence in the Lake District and on the Pennines is very similar.[1] There are some examples of circular hut bases with seemingly scooped-out interiors and no doorways. The site at Ribblehead is associated with some small plots which have curving boundary banks, and flints and animal bones have been found, but they have not been dated. Dr. Raistrick did find some pottery in the sub-circular hut on Comb Scar at Malham and suggests a Bronze Age date for it.

Alan Aberg's difficult and trying dig in the hilltop enclosure at Horse Close Farm, Skipton, revealed two huts. The larger hut, circular or possibly an oval shape, later converted into a round house, was 26 feet in diameter. It was a timber structure and in places a nine inch trench was cut into the solid millstone grit, holding the posts for the walls. They were four nine inch posts in the centre of the hut, presumably to hold up the roof. The pottery suggested a pre-Roman Iron Age date, though a Romano-British bronze dress fastening was found in the top soil. The other hut excavated was a sub-rectangular form.

Round stone walled houses, the floors level with their sur- roundings, are widely distributed and it is possible to find them in villages and in homesteads. In size they vary from a diameter of 15 feet to about 35 feet in West Yorkshire, but the enormous 50 foot example at Ewe Close in Westmorland shows clearly that some architectural principles were under- stood and large timber roof supports were available locally. The suggestion has been made that British deciduous trees were unsuitable for straight beams and so we persevered with the circular house.

Larger settlements are easier to find and will be considered first. These are hamlets with numerous houses, some connected by roads to outlying fields or a water supply. Droveways lead up on to the fellside, suggesting daily or seasonal grazing there. Having used the term hamlet it would be wise to caution readers accustomed to the later nucleated form, with the houses grouped together round a focal point. Romano- British examples tend to be strung out, and some of the smaller fields or stock pounds are almost the same size as the houses. There are no local examples to compare in size with the defended hill fort villages of the Southern Uplands of Scotland. Hilltop villages cover 40 acres at Traprain Law and Eildon Hill North, and each was a possible capital for a different tribe. On the later site 300 house floors can still be seen on the surface and a good many have been destroyed or are hidden

by trees. The field systems in Scotland are not linked to the settlements and so it is not possible without excavation to consider the way of life of the people.

The field systems north of Grassington cover about 90 acres and are the best-known examples in West Yorkshire. They stretch from north of Sweetside (SE001657) to the southern tip of High Close (SE003647), covering a hill slope that rises from about 800 feet in the west to 1,000 feet. A number of small farmsteads with rectangular huts can be found among the fields in the south and there are trackways running from them. The fields are square to rectangular, none of them covering an acre, the longer fields tend to run up the hill slope. Some of the later medieval remains no doubt cover up Romano-British sites, especially around the Cove. This draws attention to the long period of time covered by the field remains. The High Close cairn yielded a beaker with crouched burial, and on Lea Green a Bronze Age burial mound may be associated with fields of the same date.

A NATIVE SETTLEMENT AT RIBBLEHEAD
*The women are shown weaving, grinding corn
and cooking.*

Between Malham Tarn and Cowside Beck lies a settlement consisting of more huts than any other in the district. This Middlehouse site has been escavated in part by Dr. Raistrick and an account and plan published.[2] Situated on a limestone terrace facing south-east at an altitude of 1500 feet O.D. are eight large huts with diameters varying from 25 feet to 35 feet. These are free-standing huts with walls three to four feet thick. Around three sides of the hut group is a wall into which, or against which, have been built another 12 huts slightly smaller than the free-standing examples. The grouping of huts in twos and threes suggests they were not all habitations, and perhaps the smaller examples were granaries.

In Upper Ribblesdale, the settlement at Colt Park, sheltered from the west by the Ingleborough mass, has seven huts, two threes and a one. The southern holding of three huts and the central one with three are entered by well-defined gateways, with the posts remaining; those in the southern hut standing eight feet apart. A well-marked, double banked trackway about six yards wide runs along the eastern side of the farms, being re-routed at some stage around a small croft before turning east and extending downhill almost to the Ribble, a quarter of a mile to the east. Field banks dividing off areas from 12 to 15 acres in extent occur in a zone between the small crofts adjacent to the huts in the west and those of a badly robbed area below the Leeds-Carlisle railway line. Here are two large circular huts, both built against the straight croft sides in sheltered positions.

The area covered is about 70 acres, divided perhaps between five homesteads, suggesting 14 acres per family group, but the very large fields may not have been used for growing cereals. Corn would have been grown, and the number of field boundaries running across bare limestone pavements testify to extensive soil erosion. Fertile soils have been destroyed and those existing on the limestone terraces today bear little relationship to those of the Romano-British period.

Lowndes, in the report of his excavation at Ellerbeck in the Lune Valley, suggested spelt was grown.[3] Small-scale trials using barley (*Hordeum spontaneum*) and Spelt (*Triticium spelta*) have been carried out at Settle, but although the crop was left until December before harvesting, and then dried indoors in a greenhouse, only a small amount of seed corn was produced. It could be that small crofts were used for growing seed grain while larger fields produced cereals that could be dried on racks for flour.

Spelt is normally a long-strawed cereal, but this would only occur if soil fertility was high. The length of straw is a measure of the plant's ability to take up nutrients from the soil, and whatever fertilisers were used on the wet upland soils, short-strawed crops would still result. This would be an advantage at an altitude of 1100 feet O.D., where winds would be likely to flatten long-strawed growth. There would be little difference in the grain yield between good and poor soils, or between acid and alkali, and periods of fallow would be unnecessary.

The land could be expected to yield 9-11 bushels per acre, i.e. about a third of the present yields, and a third of this would need to be stored for seed. The resulting 6-8 bushels would

COLT PARK, NORTH RIBBLESDALE
*There are probably three native farmsteads seen
sheltering in the lea of the low limestone terrace.
A well defined trackway, running along the eastern
side of the farms, extends almost to the Ribble
a quarter of a mile away.*

provide enough flour or meal for a couple of people for a year, so a rule-of-thumb proportion can be worked out between field areas and population. The population could be equal to the acreage of arable land. I feel that half of Colt Park could have been ploughed, and so we could expect households of six to ten people, who need not all live in the same hut; a household may have two or three huts at its disposal.

The diet would not be all provided by the arable fields. Cattle, sheep, horses and pigs were reared and people took wild birds and their eggs. The surrounding countryside would hold game and could be expected to provide some fruit, berries, nuts and possibly fish, but this would vary with the season.

Colt Park is to be found in Ingram Lodge Shaw Pasture and the fields to the east, but previous authors have linked the site with the farm to the north and used its name. In the Ribblehead neighbourhood are over 200 acres of "Celtic fields" running at an altitude of about 1,100 feet O.D., from Gauber Limekiln Pasture to Colt Park. Hut forms in the north are not all circular.

The distribution of these Romano-British sites, and their forerunners on the Carboniferous Limestone, has been noted. As the limestone dips beneath the Yoredale Series to the north there are less extensive settlements but in Wensleydale an area is to be found on the slopes of Addlebrough. The geological map shows an area of limestone running along the southern edge of the Vale of Eden, between Kirkby Stephen and Shap and here numerous settlements are to be found. Most of them were recorded at the beginning of this century by W. G. Collingwood in the *Transactions of the Cumberland and West-morland Society*.[3]

Ewe Close was excavated by Mr. Collingwood in 1907. It is a settlement almost completely enclosed by a six feet thick double-faced boulder wall, with a rectangular plan, the western squared portion having a 50 feet circular hut at its centre. This enormous hut is most unusual and has been considered the home of a chief whose followers lived in smaller huts flanking the gateway. Three hut foundations are to be found on either side of the gateway, and other six or seven occur a little further away to the south-east. The huts at the gateway are integral parts of the gateway and thus guard chambers; this does not imply that they were copied from a Roman fort, though the squared plan surely owes something to Roman forms. The most important point is the fact that the Roman Road from Ribchester through Overburrow to Carlisle passes within 50 yards of the very large hut and appears to have gone off course by Ewe Close.

The Romans were attracted by the native settlements. There can be little doubt that the limestone uplands provided a number of commodities for the Roman legions. Brigantian cornfields would contribute a good deal of corn for the soldiers' daily ration. Meat was possibly added to the menu, as it would have been difficult to supply the more usual Roman rations— corn, wine, oil—in sufficient quantities. (Cattle bones are certainly more common than those of horse at Ribchester and Lancaster, in spite of the fact that they were cavalry forts).

As the limestone dips northwards the upper beds are at a higher level in the south of the district, near Settle, the limestone at Victoria Cave reaches an altitude of over 1,500 feet. Metalwork from this and the adjacent caves is famous and has possibly drawn attention away from surface features in the neighbourhood. Virtually on the roof of Victoria Cave are 12 circular hut bases which follow the contour; this is a hill top site with a bank running around it, but the bank has no defensive purpose. The two larger huts are over 30 feet in diameter but when excavated no architectual details other than in the wall structure were seen.

This is now an area of rough, coarse pasture used for summer grazing, with no surface water except where stock use dewponds, probably of medieval date, for a drinking supply. If present rainfall figures are similar or greater than during the period of occupation, as they appear to be from what evidence is to hand, there must have been factors outweighing the absence of water when people chose to live there.

The present ground level is below the Romano-British horizon, yet under the wall foundation were pieces of barytes with ore staining. An oval hollow, oriented east-west, contained a large quantity of barytes, which must be considered a gangue or vein mineral, and a fair amount of the two copper carbonates was present. Below the mineral deposit lay a small amount of slag. The hollow was lined with clay which appeared to have been puddled into the bottom to make a bowl furnace.

The evidence for metalworking is very slight but is considered reasonable in an ore-bearing locality. It is hoped that the future detailed analyses of lead, bronze and silver will become available; without them it will be impossible to look closely at the different metalworking schools of Highland Britain during the first three centuries A.D. Excavation may produce evidence like the fine clay moulds from Traprain Law, in West Lothian.

A reconstruction of the Victoria site cannot show the bronzes

that may have been produced because of the scale  Examples
drawn from the caves would have been produced with the
same technological facilities. The "Lost Wax" technique of
casting and the fine *champlevé* method of enamelling contrast
with rude living conditions, but we probably have a superior
attitude when considering the past.

There seems to be an end to the native metalworking about
150 A.D., which coincides with uprisings in Brigantia and the
sacking and destruction of many Roman forts. The period of
Roman rebuilding that followed would surely have seen many
previously free men working for the Romans. The smiths
may also have been conscripted into service and it is interesting to note the late evidence for bronze-working in the
fort principia at Bainbridge.

A NATIVE VILLAGE OF THE ROMAN PERIOD
*Showing mineral working, crushing and smelting.*

Settlements mentioned have been circular-hutted types on the terraces of the Great Scar Limestone. The geology map is too small in scale for walkers but it should aid motorists in their hunt for the settlement level. A noteworthy exception is a small site at Helwith Bridge. The site can be found on the eastern valley side and comprises two portions. The higher eastern part on the steeper-sloping terrain has two hut circles, 25 and 35 feet in diameter respectively, together with stock pounds and some small plots. On the lower ground is an almost rectangular enclosure surrounded by a six feet thick double-boulder faced wall (see site plan).

On the field surface were found at least a dozen millstone grit rotary quernstones and the inhabitants of the site were more than farmers. Grit boulders washed out of the boulder clay "tail" south of Penyghent are the raw material. These could be easily broken in half and then the upper stone could be drilled to give the corn hopper, feed tube and, on another boring, the handle hole. The lower stones were pierced by a small hole, enough to take an iron pin around which the quern rotates. A chunk was usually knocked off the bottom to make it stand firm.

A trackway for transporting the goods must be nearby as the two stones together weigh over 75 pounds. It is likely that Mastiles Lane, the trackway across Malham Moor, divided in the west, one part dropping into Stainforth and crossing the Ribble and the other extending northward slightly to a ford very close to the site at Helwith Bridge. The earliest pottery found here was a sherd of late Second century Samaian ware, and the most recent was a piece of a vessel possibly made locally sometime in the Fourth century. I have attempted to date examples of circular huts over the district as a whole.

QUERNS

CORN HOPPER ↓

HANDLE SOCKET

FLOUR →

IRON PIN

LATER ROMAN FORM.

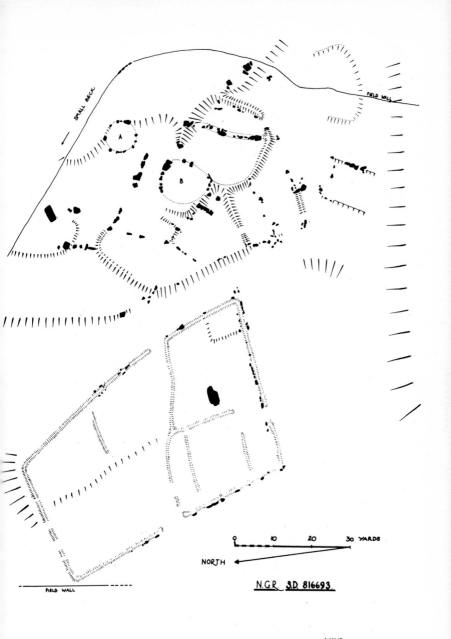

NATIVE FARMSTEAD, HELWITH BRIDGE

It must be pointed out that almost as many settlements exist with rectangular huts, and it is possible to find both forms together on one site. Two rectangular hut platforms can be found in the corners of the lower rectangular enclosure at Helwith Bridge.

A scheduled site a little downstream, on the opposite side of the valley, beneath Smearsett Hill, has two rectangular hut platforms each about 30 feet by 12 feet. Close to the huts are some small garden-sized rectangular plots and, further away and running up the valley side, exist a series of long strip fields without lynchets; in all the site covers about 24 acres. Excavation here yielded no dateable material.

Extensive settlements with rectangular huts can be found in Gauber Cow Pasture and in Gauber Limekiln Pasture at Ribblehead. These settlements extend intermittently down Chapel-le-Dale valley, the finds normally indicating an occupation during the later part of the Roman period.

In Westmorland the hut forms vary from circular to square and rectangular. The most common shape is round, the huts being built into the field or enclosure walls. At Wickerslack Moor the round huts are set into the hillside at the break of the slope but Kentmere has five free-standing circular huts inside a thick boulder faced wall, and at least one of these was occupied during the Second century. There are places in Westmorland that compare almost indentically with examples in the Dales, Ewe Locks, with a bipartite appearance, readily brings the Helwith Bridge site to mind. In Wharfedale the settlement at the northern end of Lea Green has numerous rectangular huts inside an enclosing wall. The inhabitants of this site were probably folk who farmed the extensive fields to the south-east.

On most of the West Craven sites where rectangular huts are found with circular ones, the circular ones are quite small, about 15 feet in diameter, suggesting that when the circular form was no longer fashionable as a dwelling it was maintained as an outhouse, perhaps as a granary. There is therefore a suggestion of a later date for the rectangular huts, but people were certainly living in both forms at the same time. The rectangular form is only found after the Roman invasion of the north, rare examples of circular buildings built in stone clearly predate the Romans. The circular stone form must have evolved from the earlier timber hut.

Can the single rectangular huts that are intrusive elements at Ewe Close, Colt Park and Victoria be taken as evidence of the Roman control of the native population? The larger

**PART OF THE NATIVE FARMSTEAD
BELOW SMEARSETT**
*The small enclosures lie above a rectangular
hut platform, and long strip fields about 15 yards
wide extend up the hillside.*

centres may have merited an overseer, especially (as has been stated earlier) when they were contributing cereals and other goods for the Roman army. Prof. Piggott has suggested that the Greek and Roman armies had a cereal ration of about ten bushels per head per year, and earlier it was considered that some meat may have augmented their diet. Many writers have commented on the diet of the Celts, with Diodorus Siculus referring to blazing fires with cauldrons and spits loaded with great joints of meat. Roman authors considering the greed of the Celts were underlining a fundamental difference in diet between two European cultures from totally differing native environments.

The Roman's food was based on the products of the Mediterranean lands, with vegetable oil and grain the staple items. The Celts ate more meat. Prof. Jackson describes the food served at the Irish feasts; this was chiefly meat, beef veal and, above all, pork.[5] Whole roast pigs were carved up and there was meat in cauldrons. Cakes of flour were baked with honey. The Irish evidence is used because the Romans never landed there; so the Iron Age, the heroic period of the Irish tales, is preserved in writing, though stories and descriptions were written down centuries after they were delivered to their first audiences.

There is ample evidence on the Romano-British sites for the rearing of cattle, sheep, horses and pigs. Butchers knives and at least one fine cauldron have been discovered. We know that British textiles were valued throughout the Roman Empire, and whilst the State interest in the woollen industry is considered a late development, the fame of it had been achieved before the year 301, when Diocletian's edict was made known.

The Roman conquest of the greater part of Brigantia, which was fundamentally the upland Pennine area, was completed by Petillius Cerialis in 71-74 A.D. We know that the tribe had split into pro-Roman and anti-Roman fractions, possibly in the year 47 A.D., which was unfortunate, for Caratacus who, having seen his army of Silures defeated somewhere on the Welsh Borders, possibly in Shropshire, sought help and protection in Yorkshire but was put in chains and handed over to the Romans by Cartimandua, Queen of the Brigantes. Sir Mortimer Wheeler and others have suggested that Cartimandua was not a native of the north, and her personality had been shaped elsewhere. Whatever her origins, the break-up of her marriage with Venutius became the occasion of a tribal war, only Roman interference saving her.

While the Brigantes were at peace they formed a fine buffer

between the Romans and the kingdoms in Scotland, but armed they were a possible source of trouble. Venutius was the obvious choice of leader for native resistance. Cerialis attacked and "after a series of battles, some not uncostly, Petillius had operated, if not actually triumphed, over the major part of their territory." Sir Mortimer Wheeler after excavating the fort at Stanwick, about six miles north of Richmond, in the North Riding, considered the evidence impressive enough to suggest the site was the battlefield between the Brigantes and the Ninth Legion from York. A chariot burial which had previously been found may even mark the grave of Venutius.

Cerialis' term of office ended in 74 AD and the Brigantes were to remain unharried for about five years. Agricola, possibly the most famous of the governors of Britain, arrived in the summer of 78 and he fought and virtually destroyed the Ordovices of North Wales in the same year; in 79 he advanced northwards, probably along the west coast route.The legionary fortress at Chester can be envisaged as the starting point for his expeditions, the sites for the Manchester, Ribchester, Elslack, Overborough and possibly the Lancaster fort being chosen at this time and built normally in turf and timber. Forces may have moved north from York at the same time, contact being made through the Pennine valleys. A road network built for strategic reasons brought internal security and traders. The Pax Romana had to be paid for, and unless we accept that the natives were already working lead in the Grassington-Pateley Bridge area the Romans quickly established mines; two lead ingots or pigs found at Hayshaw Bank can be dated to the years 81 or 82 AD.

The motorist and general reader should try to acquire one of the Ordnance Survey maps of Roman Britain, for although they are of small scale it is possible to use them in conjunction with a 1ins sheet and find the uncovered stretches of Roman Road. Naturally the first civil engineers in the north-west chose the obvious routes from the direct Manchester-Blackburn-Ribchester stretches to the picturesque Ribchester-Slaidburn-Overburrow drive. The newly-built Whalley-Clitheroe by-pass near Worston runs alongside the Roman road from Ribchester to Elslack, now in an avenue of beech trees, before covering it up to the north.(At a time when milestones are about to be replaced by kilometre-markers mention should be made of the late Roman example, 300 yards south of the church at Middleton on Lune, between Kirkby Lonsdale and Sedbergh. The number LIII possibly refers to the distance, 53 miles, to Carlisle.)

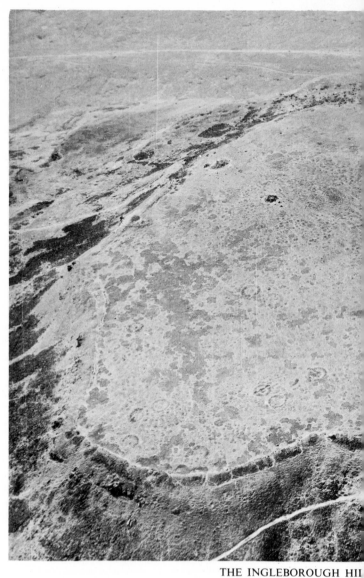

THE INGLEBOROUGH HI[

RT FROM THE NORTH-EAST.

*Circular huts are seen scattered over the plateau which is bounded by a dry-stone wall.*

It is often written that the Brigantes who escaped from Stanwick fled into the Dales and set up strongholds on Ingleborough, at Far Gregory in Upper Wharfedale and on Carrock Fell. This may in time prove to be so but there is at present no evidence. When these three forts are considered with the Roman Road network the suggestion must be that they were not built after the road system was completed, so a pre-Agricolan date is most likely.

The Ingleborough summit, situated at a height over 2373 feet, must be one of the most inhospitable sites in the Pennines and it is difficult to imagine a permanent settlement either here or on Carrock Fell. Ingleborough is most imposing from the west, being visible from any of the drumlins in Lonsdale and even from the site of the Roman fort in Lancaster, which is now partly covered by the castle and priory church.

On Ingleborough a stone wall surrounds a 16 acre triangular plateau. The strength of the wall is not constant, and is even absent in places, but the "gaps" do not prove that the Romans knocked down or removed stretches of the wall. In places the

*Below: A reconstruction of the Ingleborough hill fort wall.*

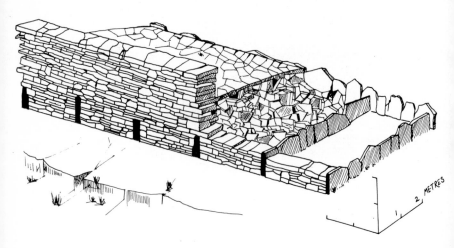

2 METRES

sheer cliffs would be a good enough for defence. Fourteen foot thick, the outer face of the wall is coursed gritstones, and showing the ends of vertically aligned "throughs" which divide the wall into compartments filled with rubble and comparable with structures on the Continent. In South Germany a hill fort at Priest had timber beams passing through the stone face and through the earth and rubble fill, "analogous to the bulk-heads of a ships hull so decreasing the danger of collapse." Beams would bind together a rampart with a proportion of earth in it, but the features on Ingleborough only strengthen it if there is the likelihood of lateral rubble movement, so a rampart walk is envisaged; otherwise the builders were trying to do in stone what they were used to doing where timber was more plentiful. The wall must be considered earlier than the Roman campaign by Agricola but there is every likelihood that it had a periodic life during the later periods of unrest. An aerial photo-graph shows circular hut foundations from 24 feet to 34 feet in diameter, the majority being about 30 feet. These can be matched at lower levels on the limestone with huts occupied during the Roman occupation. The only pottery sherd known to the writer to have come from the fort area must be dated to the third or fourth century, and if this is the date of the visible hut foundations then earlier structures are maybe hidden

We return to the Roman forts to find evidence of the Brigantian uprisings, and it cannot be coincidence that the South Gateways into Elslack and Overburrow forts were destroyed by fire together with the initial timber villa at Gargrave. There is the suggestion at Bainbridge of a series of native revolts during the Second century. At Elslack reddened clay was found, with burnt sandstone around the top of postholes, and in 15 out of 18 post holes the stumps of the timbers remained. Finely-preserved timbering, some posts measuring 10 ins. x 16 ins., and evidence of destruction by fire, were found at Lancaster, it being assumed that the evidence is earlier than the stone fort. A problem of the Brigantian uprising is the extent of the support received from the tribes of Scotland. We do know that the turf-built Antonine Wall was destroyed with its forts and with the loss of almost all the forts in the Scottish lowlands. The expansionist era of empire building was over; the Romans left Scotland to crush the Brigantes and to consolidate their holdings in northern England.

Rebuilding usually took place in stone and often inscriptions help to date the masonry. Ilkley was re-occupied by 169 AD. The Sarmatian cavalry, some of whom occupied Ribchester, were not moved from the Continent until 175 AD. Elslack and Bainbridge, too, were re-occupied. An inscription from Church Street in Lancaster suggests that buildings had been allowed to decay, and the rebuilding of a basilica by the Sebusian cavalry is dated to the year 262.

Forts were strengthened and cavalry made the policing of the area a simpler task. Severus and his sons Caracalla and Geta campaigned in Scotland early in the Third century, bringing about the surrender of the Caledonians in 209 and the Maeatae in 210. Severus died at York while preparing for another season's warfare and it is clear that York was the administrative centre for the north at this time; it was far more than a fortress. A large civil settlement had grown up at York and the Severan reforms allowing legionary soldiers to marry, and the grants of land to soldiers, helped to create a peaceful period which lasted almost a century in the north. An inscription at Ribchester records the granting of land to the Sarmatian veterans. They had been serving here for possibly 35 years and by settling them locally the military were creating a reserve.

Life on the native farmsteads changed little, though many men and sons would be conscripted into army service. Goods of Roman origin are rare, a few Samian bowls gracing the hearths, but coins are frequently found. A coin hoard from a camp bordering Attermire cannot have been hidden in its pot before the opening of the Fourth century; the hut in which it was found had been burnt down.

The wealth of the north was again attracting invaders, and lands bordering the Irish Sea were troubled by raiders from Ireland or South-West Scotland. About 367 there was a conspiracy of invaders and attacks were made by Franks, Saxons in the east and by the Picts and Scots in the west. The breakdown of barriers between the soldiers and the natives, through intermarriage and soldiers taking up farming, possibly wanting to forget drill and discipline, had created a lax defensive system. New methods were evolved, and foremost among them was an early warning signalling system along the cliffs of North Yorkshire.

The native tribes were now to attempt their own defence and the life of the fort at Overborough was ended. The principia at Bainbridge was not rebuilt after it had been burned down about 367, but occupation continued, as shown by Mr. Hartley's recent excavations. Time and again leaders of the army crossed the Channel to annexe Gaul, and a buffer was needed to prevent invasion from the continent by the barbarians. Britain

**ROMAN FORT AT BAINBRIDGE**
*The photograph shows the latest fort
built over the clearly marked earlier defences.*

could ill afford the drain of troops in the 380s by Magnus Maximus, and in 407 by Constantine II, especially as both men were overthrown when they attempted to interfere in Italy and their troops deployed to defend Rome.

Independence was not gained by the defeat of the Romans by British forces; it was simply that Rome could no longer defend Britain. Ironically, the country was Romanised and recent excavations at York Minster have shown that the city was still in its Roman state when King Edwin was baptized there in 627. The enemies from across the seas were now considered to be the barbarians, and when Aneirin, in his ancient Celtic elegy, praised the 300 warriors assembled in Edinburgh to fight the Saxons, he described their heavy Roman armour and their way of fighting from horseback with javelins and spears.[7] An even greater irony was the fact that this small Sixth century cavalry regiment paid for their year of feasting with their lives at Catterick, near the site at Stanwick where the Brigantes had fought in 74 AD.

1. Jobey, G.—"Homesteads and Settlements of the Frontier Area" in Rural Settlement in Roman Britain, ed. Thomas, C. (1966).
   This book is a series of papers given at a conference in Oxford in 1965 and is well worth reading.
2. Raistrick, A., and Holmes, P. F.—"Archæology of Malham Moor," Field Studies, Vol I, No. 4 (1962).
3. Lowndes, R. A. C.—"Excavations of a Romano-British Farmstead at Ellerbeck," Trans. Cumb. & Westmorland Antiq. & Archaeol. Soc. Vol. LXIV 6-28 (1964).
5. Collingwood, R. G.—"Prehistoric Settlement near Crosby Ravensworth", Trans. Cumb. & Westmorland Antiq. and Archaeol. Soc., Vol. XXXIII, 201-226 (1933).
6. Wheeler, M.—"The Stanwick Fortifications," Research Report 17, Soc. of Antiquaries, (1954).

# 7. The Post-Roman Period

ISOLATED and drained of resources, in particular of soldiers, the peoples of Britain found themselves cut off from their fellow Christians by a wedge of paganism stretching southwards from the Germanic lands. The tribal leaders, most of them with some knowledge of Latin, were conscious of the Romanisation that had occurred in their lands during the occupation. Brigantia as a kingdom was ended centuries ago, and now the North had to try to defend itself against the Anglo-Saxons. It is likely that the North came under their influence as much by the revolt of the mercenaries brought in to defend our shores as by actual invasion and conquest. The east coast had in late Roman times been equipped with forts and signal stations to give warning of sea-borne attack, but quickly these coastlands were settled by the Anglo-Saxons.

The Angles came from the southern part of what is now Denmark and the Saxons from neighbouring North Germany and Holland, while the Jutes who settled in Kent and the Channel area came from Jutland. There were no doubt Frisians from North Holland and the off-shore islands, as suggested by some of the placenames, e.g. Monk Fryston. (Friesian cattle are a much more recent introduction). The north slowly developed new characteristics and these are described as Anglian.

From a study of burials and graves, Mr. E. T. Leeds has shown that the Anglo-Saxon cemeteries have no relationship to the Roman road system and the Anglo-Saxons generally avoided the existing towns and forts. Their routeways, from material and place-name evidence, were the river valleys, and the mobile troops of knights, (even when lead by "King" Arthur) failed to stop them. Arthur was not king in the accepted sense of the term, but he does appear to have been the leader of the army or at least the cavalry. It is clear that no new tactics were evolved after the defeat at Catreath or Catterick.

In the North-West, Urien ruled his kingdom of Rheged or Strathclyde, stretching from South-West Scotland through the Lake Counties to North Lancashire, and across West Yorkshire to where the dales valleys exit from the eastern Pennines. Mr. A. H. A. Hogg has tried to locate the centre of this kingdom and suggests that its capital, Lluyuenyd, could be associated with the river Lyvennet, a tributary of the Upper Eden off the limestone district of Crosby Ravensworth. Urien and his sons joined in battle against the Saxons at Lindisfarne about the year 590. It is difficult to say whether the battle of Chester, about 615 AD, followed the defeat of the Britons at Catterick or preceded it. These two battles opened up the routes into the Pennine areas and into Lancashire from the south.

We have moved away from fieldwork and field evidence but this is the effect of moving into the historic period where literary work is available. Bede's *History of the English Church* in particular contains a great deal of material illuminating life of the period.[1] Bede was not born until 673, but as a monk living out his life at Wearmouth and Jarrow he was able to document fairly accurately events that had occurred before his birth. The church was divided, for with the withdrawal of the Roman forces and the contraction of the Empire, the Celtic Church in the west evolved independently from the Roman Church. This was the period of Ninian, Patrick, Columba and David the Footloose, learned Celtic saints. Their church was organised on a monastic basis with the bishops working to the suggestions of their abbot. Bede suggests they wished the Anglo-Saxons eternal damnation.

The Augustine mission to Britain on behalf of the Roman church began in 596, with Augustine landing in Kent the following year. Understandably the Celtic bishops at their meeting with him at Bangor (is y coed?) would not recognize him as their archbishop, and it was not until the Synod of Whitby in 664 that a degree of church unity was achieved. Bishop Wilfred was given a monastery and land in Ripon in that year, Alfred (the donor) preferring the Roman faith, while his father Oswy followed Celtic ways.

Missionaries set up crosses at preaching points, an act that hallowed the site. It is likely that the sites were enclosed, and churches were built on many of them. Adamnan, writing about St. Columba, says that a cross was set up on Iona to mark the spot where Columba sat down on his last walk and to mark a farewell to the old white horse. The cross was stuck in the top of a quern and was obviously only a light wooden form. Missionaries may well have used their staffs.

Military, political or economic strength must come before any development of the arts, and from the beginning of the Sixth century to the close of the Eighth the kingdoms of Northumbria—i.e. the land north of the Humber—and Mercia became individually powerful. Northumbrian kings, Edwin, Oswald and Oswy, came close to being kings of England in the early Seventh century, but power slowly drifted south, first to Mercia, under Aethelbald and later Offa, and then to Wessex.

The forging of a Northumbrian "nation" meant that craftsmen in particular masons were drawn to the centres of government and learning. The wooden crosses were copied in stone using carpentery techniques. Collingwood considers the death of Bishop Acca in 740 "the moment for genius to rise", and believes the stone crosses of north Lancashire, with their stylized bunches of grapes, originated artistically in the Hexham district.[2] Examples, usually preserved inside the parish churches, can be found at Heysham, Halton-on-Lune, Kendal and at Heversham. A fine shaft top at Hornby, which shows the Miracle of the Loaves and Fishes, showed the two apostles above five loaves and two not-so-small fish. From the plaiting on the reverse this has been linked to the Ripon school of cross design.

In West Yorkshire too the crosses are worthy of consideration. At Otley are two portions of shaft, with beautifully carved figures, the larger panel showing a monk in profile kneeling at the feet of a winged angel. There is the basal part of another shaft. Three Anglian crosses can be seen in Ilkley church and one cross survives at Kildwick. They have all free-armed heads, and it is unlikely that they were erected before the Ninth century. About this time a church dedicated to St. Peter was built at Heysham.

A study of the crosses and associated buildings, where they exist, entails a good deal of travel but produces a picture of the Anglian spread across the north of England. A similar result should be obtained by a study of the placenames on any map, (a selection of placename elements appears in Appendix 1). The more detailed and larger the scale of the map the more likely it is that the older names will be in evidence, for these are usually the topographical features. The villages of the Dales often retain the outline of their Anglian form, nucleated around a green, sometimes with a church at one end, similar

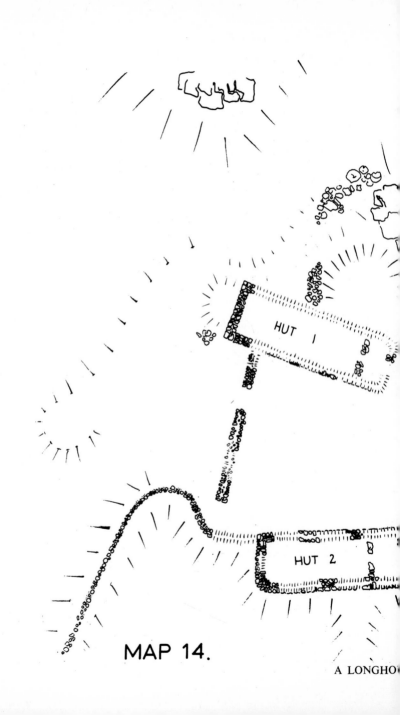

HUT 1

HUT 2

MAP 14.

A LONGHO

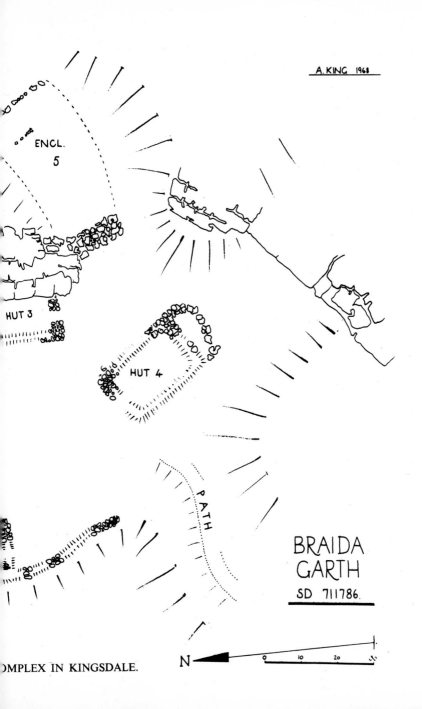

A. KING 1968

ENCL. 5

HUT 3

HUT 4

PATH

BRAIDA GARTH

SD 711786.

N

0     10     20     30

OMPLEX IN KINGSDALE.

*Viking bowl of silver, found on Halton Moor, Lonsdale. (British Museum).*

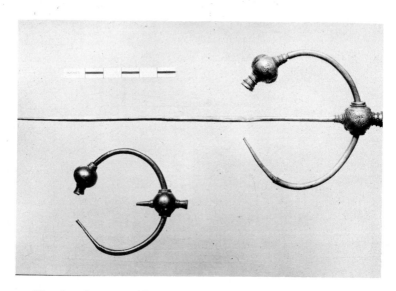

*Silver brooches of the Viking period, from Hutton-in-the-forest and Casterton. (Tullie House, Carlisle).*

to examples in north Germany. They appear less frequently in Lancashire, though examples are to be found in the north of the county.

Taken together, the place-names, the crosses and the rare archaeological finds, such as the sword pommel from Ingleton, mark out the lines of Anglian penetration into and through the Pennines. The heavier iron tools, axes in particular, were being used to clear the valley floors, and ploughs were breaking new ground. Progress and peace in the country came to a temporary end in 787 with the first of the Viking raids.

According to the chronicles in that year "came first three ships of Norwegians . . . and the reeve rode thither and tried to compel them to go to the royal manor, for he did not know what they were, and they slew him." Lindisfarne monastery was destroyed in 793, and Jarrow was looted the following year. The heathen Vikings, Danes or Northmen increased their raids and possibly began to settle, but it was not until Alfred ended their run of battle victories in 878 that the Vikings were established with their own land.

Viking raiders in wooden longboats came directly to the east coast. To go viking was to go raiding, using a boat about 70 feet long with a crew of up to 70. Their fellows were then sailing to Iceland, Greenland and on to the eastern seaboard of North America. They were settling in the Scottish Isles and in Ireland and when these settlers, generations later, raided the North-West of England they were called Norse. These were the people who rededicated the small church at Heysham to St. Patrick and buried their dead under the hog-back tombs. These tombs are considered to be small replicas of their own long houses, boat-shaped in plan with a piched roof possibly covered in shingles. There are two fine examples at Gosforth, the more realistic shape having a multitude of warriors carved along one side. Other examples can be seen at Lowther, and there is one in the parish church at Burnsall.

The Norse influence was greatest in Lonsdale and Kentdale, and it continued eastward into the Yorkshire Dales. Eventually a kingdom existed, being ruled from Dublin and York but it was shortlived, ending with the death of Eric Bloodaxe in Stainmore in 954. This influence can be seen in some of the crosses of the district. A fine shaft with panels of Norse mythology stands in the churchyard at Halton-on-Lune. One shows Sigurd the Volsung forging a sword; also the bodies of Fafni and dragon and Regni the smith. The lower panel shows Sigurd roasting the dragon's heart and licking his burnt or smarting fingers. The taste of dragon's blood had the magical

VIKING MYTHOLOGY: SHOWN ON A SWEDISH
ROCK-CARVING
(*to be compared with the Viking cross shaft
at Halton-on-Lune*).

*Sigurd, with the sword, kills the dragon Fafnir.*
*In the centre, Sigurd is seen roasting Fafnir's heart over*
*a fire. When Sigurd licked his thumb he tasted dragon's*
*blood and was able to understand the warnings of the*
*birds. Regin, the evil smith, is beheaded.*

effect of giving Sigurd an understanding of bird's voices. Placenames with a strong Norse element are most common on the hills and wilder country, which suggests that the latest group of invaders settled on land ignored by the Angles. The district between Settle and Sedbergh has between 60 and 70% of the placenames of this origin.

It remains for us to identify and excavate a Norse settlement, which must surely be found. Discoveries like a huge silver brooch at Casterton (a brooch now in Tullie House, Carlisle) and silver bowl found at Halton-on-Lune and now in the British Museum, cannot have existed in isolation. Mr. Lamb working from historical information at the Meteorological Office suggests that the climate between 1,000 and 1,200 AD had summer temperatures perhaps 1°C. above the present figures with slightly lower rainfall, so settlement can be expected at slightly higher altitudes than at present, assuming there is a reliable water supply. The limestone terraces and ghylls, including those facing the north, would compare favourably with settlement sites in Norway or Iceland.

Long huts are to be found with, or at slightly higher levels than the Romano-British settlements, in Penyghent Ghyll, at Ribblehead, in Crummackdale, Clapdale and at Braida Garth in Kingsdale. Only the longest have been mentioned. An example in Gauber High Pasture, backed by about three acres of arable field systems, is 68 feet by 18 feet with a doorway off centre and in the northern gable. This suggests a roof pillar in a central position, with others possibly along the axis of the hut supporting a pitched roof.

The site at Braida Garth, at an altitude of 1,000 feet has a 50 feet long hut with a dividing wall and a stone slab that could easily be a boskin or stall divider. The double-faced dry stone walls are about two foot thick, built of slabby limestone blocks. The smallest of the huts is positioned below what is, on occasion a waterfall. This suggests that the climate was less wet than at the present time.

A long hut has been excavated at Millhouse in Lunesdale, and Lowndes was able to date the occupation to the thirteenth and fourteenth centuries. It is not felt this one example should be used to suggest a Medieval date for all long huts, but clearly any information is a positive step.

This pastoral area should not fail to interest fieldworkers, for the landscape with its prehistoric scars, is a palimpsest drawn out on a geological foundation that is still posing questions for students at all levels. This is the major advantage of the area. Any teacher can find a vast range of problems for students. The study can be one of minute detail or for any period of time it can be incorporated into a national scheme. Each parish, every village, contains quantities of rewarding information. The Anglian nucleated settlements must be considered with their strip fields and out-field areas. But let us remember that the field evidence is the carefully-recorded past of people and their environmental problems. The success or failure of their harvests, the cattle diseases and intermarriage, must eventually enter our analysis and add meaning to any study.

By understanding the fact that changes are inevitable, no matter how slowly they occur, we should be able to plan a future.

1. *Bede—"A History of the English Church and People", Penguin* (1955).
2. *Collingwood, R. G.—"Northumbrian Crosses of the pre-Norman era".*
3. *Lamb, H. H.—"The Changing Climate"* (1966).
   *Various editions exist of "The Anglo Saxon Chronicles" and these complement Bede's work. The English Place-name Society has published volumes on both the West Riding and Westmorland by A. H. Smith. For this study in Lancashire see "Place-names of Lancashire," by E. Ekwall, Manchester* (1922).

# An Introduction to Place Names

PLACE names are initially descriptive terms which quickly become proper names. In England at the present time there is little or no interest taken in the meaning of the names because of language changes.

Obsolete terms and languages will be found in these place names, a small proportion of which originated well before the birth of Christ in the pre-Celtic era. These are followed by Celtic terms, and certainly some Roman influence would have lasted into the 6th Century A.D. It seems likely that many "eccles" names, (Eccles, Eccleston, Ecclefechan) derive from the early Celtic "egles" (church); but in addition it is interesting to note their distribution very close to major Roman roads; Eccleshill, Darwen, is a good example. Here language and position help to date the spread of Christianity in the north.

Anglo-Saxon kingdoms were established, with the Anglian element being strongest in the north of England. Scandinavian terms came into use late in the 9th Century when viking raiders and settlers came onto the east coast direct from Norway and Denmark. But in the west coast areas south from Galloway to the Mersey, the influence of the raiders was indirect, coming via Ireland: this it is called Norse.

The Norman element is not very important in place names though they did "plant" castles such as Clitheroe, which developed into towns. More recently ecclesiastical Latin names and also Biblical and foreign introductions appeared. Israel and Rome can be found close together south-west of Giggleswick. Many names will have changed in spelling over the years, and the most difficult part of the study is finding the original spelling.

York was known as EBORACUM to the Romans; the "acum" means the property of - Ebor, and this could be a Celtic-sounding name not unlike Ifor; there may have been a pre-Roman British settlement on the site. When the Angles conquered the district their name for York was Eoforwik; "eofor" meant wild boar and "wik" a settlement. In the 10th Century, York was a seat of the Scandinavian kingdom and to the Norse people "eofor" meant nothing, but "jor" made sense being the word for a stallion, so Eoforwik became Jorvik. In almost a thousand years the spelling has changed again and the word has become meaningless, but most place names can be broken down and the various influences in a region can be isolated.

In the Yorkshire Dales the Norse influence is particularly strong, decreasing towards the Vale of York. It is strongest on the moors and hillsides while the Anglian or Old English names are concentrated in valley bottoms. In the following list the more common elements are given as an introduction to another facet of map work:

Abbreviations. OE—Old English; ME—Modern English; ON—Old Norse; D—Danish; OF—Old French; OS—Old Scandinavian: W—Welsh.

| a | — ON | river; Greta |
|---|------|-------------|
| austr | — ON | east; Austwick |
| beorc | — OE | birch tree, birk |
| beorg | — OE | hill or knoll; Castleberg, Norber, Gawber |
| berg | — ON | ,, ,, ,, |
| both | — OD | booth, temporary shelter |
| brakin | — ON | bracken, fern |
| broc | — OE | brook; Keldbrook |
| bur | — OE | cottage, dwelling; ON storehouse |
| burgaesn | — OE | burial place; Borrans |
| burh | — OE | fortification, earthwork, hence borough |
| burhtun | — OE | fortified farmstead; Burton |
| by | — ON | farmstead, village; Flasby, Formby, Newby |
| byre | — OE | cowshed |
| cald | — OE | cold, cool; Cold Cotes. ON- kaldr |
| caled | — W | rapid; River Calder |
| cefn | — W | ridge or back; Otley Chevin |
| cloh | — OE | dell, ravine, clough; Mere Clough |
| clos | — OF | enclosure; Great Close |
| cot | — OE | shed, cottage; Gisburn Cotes |
| croft | — OE | croft, small enclosure; Beecroft |
| cweorn | — OE | quern; Whernside |
| cwicen | — OE | mountain ash; Quicken Hole |
| dal | — OE | share of land; Kendal |
| dael | — OE | valley, dale. ON - dalr |
| dowker | — ME | diver; Dowk Cave |
| eng | — ON | water meadow; ing; Ingfield |
| feld | — OE | open country, field; fell |
| ford | — OE | ford; Stainforth, Arnford |
| fors | — ON | waterfall; Scaleber Force |
| gardr | — ON | yard, garth; Braida Garth |

93

| | | |
|---|---|---|
| gill | — OS | ravine; long Gill |
| griss | — ON | young pig; Grizedales |
| ham | — OE | homestead; Clapham |
| haugr | — ON | hill, mound; Haw, Hawber |
| hebble | — ME | footbridge (dialect) |
| hladn | — ON | barn; Laith, Laithe |
| hlaw | — OE | mound; Lowe, Law |
| holmr | — ON | water meadow; Holme |
| huin | — ON | gorse, Whinns; Whinfell |
| hypping | — OE | stepping stones; Hippin; Hipping |
| ingas | — OE | folk name suffix; Bingley |
| ingle | — ME | fire; Ingleborough |
| jarl | — ON | nobleman, earl; Yarlsber |
| kelda | — ON | spring, well; Keld, Alkelda? |
| kirkja | — ON | church; Kirkby |
| kjarr | — ON | marsh; Carr |
| lang | — OE | long; Langcliffe |
| leah | — OE | wood, clearing in the wood; Anley |
| maerc | — OE | boundary; Mearbeck, High Mark |
| main | — ME | demesne, land; The Mains |
| mor | — OE | (also ON) moor; Burn Moor |
| mor | — W | sea; Morecambe |
| rod | — OE | clearing, royd |
| rydding | — OE | clearing, Riddings |
| scaega | — OE | copse, "shaw"; Ellershaw, Oakenshaw |
| skali | — OS | hut, shed; Scaleber, Winskill |
| sker | — ON | scar; Langscar |
| stan | — OE | stone; Stainforth |
| stede | — OE | site of building, stead; Halstead |
| topt | — ON | enclosure, toft |
| tun | — OE | ton, village; Airton, Bolton |
| thorp | — D | (also ON) secondary or outlying farmstead |
| thwait | — ON | clearing, meadow |
| wic | — OE | dwelling, building, farm, Giggleswick |

The English Placename Society has produced volumes dealing with many counties. The West Riding is Volume XXXVI by A. H. Smith and is published by Cambridge University Press. Also helpful is *The Place Names of Lancashire,* by E. Ekwall, published in Manchester in 1922.

# Grid References

Unless otherwise stated the references are all in the National Grid 100Km. square SD.

**Caves.**

| | |
|---|---|
| Attermire | 850641 |
| Dowkerbottom | 952689 |
| Elbolton SE | 008616 |
| Kilnsey | 804657 |
| Lesser Kelco | 810646 |
| Victoria | 838650 |

**Burial Mounds.**

| | |
|---|---|
| Apronful of Stones, Kingsdale | 708786 |
| Bordley Stone Circle | 949653 |
| Giant's Grave | 856732 |
| Lingber Hill | 872572 |
| Sleight's Pasture | 758784 |
| Stackhouse | 812655 |

**Romano-British sites.**

Settlements exist **north of Grassington,** at the Cove SE 000650 to Lea Green 996663, with the very extensive area of Celtic fields to the east, especially in High Close SE 003647. Also, Gregory 988684, Chester Wood 984644.

**North of Malham,** astride the eastern road to the Tarn, Celtic fields and huts are to be found above the 1000ft. contour. Shorkley Hill 902638 is possibly the best viewpoint for seeing Celtic fields below the Cove, some of which have been ploughed out.

Also sites at Middlehouse 901681, Blue Scar 933708.

**Near Settle,** Victoria Camp 842652; Attermire East 846641; Helwith Bridge 816694; Smearsett 806681.

**Near Ribblehead,** Colt Park 777775 north to Gauber Lime Kiln. Pasture 764787.

**Wensleydale,** Addleborough 950869.

**Westmorland,**

| | | |
|---|---|---|
| Crosby Garrett | – Severals | NY 719064 |
| Crosby Ravensworth | Ewe Close | NY 609135 |
| Waitby Intake | NY 753077 | |
| Wickerslack Moor | NY 599156 | |

**Hill top sites**

| | | |
|---|---|---|
| Lancs. | Portfield, Whalley | 746355 |
| | Castercliff, Nelson | 885384 |
| | Wharton Crags | 492728 |
| Yorks. | Ingleborough | 741746 |
| | Sharphaw | 959553 |
| | Horse Close, Skipton | SE 000505 |

**Roman sites.**

| | | | |
|---|---|---|---|
| Bainbridge | SE 396903 | Lancaster | 473620 |
| Elslack "Burwen Cas" | 924495 | Mastiles Lane | 920655 |
| Ilkley | SE 116478 | Ribchester | 649350 |

95

*Small squared Celtic fields near Stackhouse, Settle.*

*Medieval lynchetted strip fields, Settle.*